W9-BJN-511

Werner and Susanne Lantermann

Amazon Parrots

Acclimation, Care, Diet, Diseases, Breeding
Special Chapter: Understanding Amazons

Translated from the German by
Elizabeth D. Crawford

American Advisory Editor: Matthew M. Vriends, PhD

With Color Photographs by Well-Known Animal Photographers
and Drawings by Fritz W. Köhler

BARRON'S

English translation ©Copyright 1988
by Barron's Educational Series, Inc.

©Copyright 1987 by Gräfe and Unzer
GmbH, Munich, West Germany
The title of the German book is *Amazonen*.
Translated by Elizabeth D. Crawford.

All inquiries should be addressed to:
Barron's Educational Series, Inc.
250 Wireless Boulevard
Hauppauge, NY 11788

Library of Congress Catalog Card No. 88-24061

International Standard Book No. 0-8120-4035-X

Library of Congress Cataloging-in-Publication Data

Lantermann, Werner, 1956 —
    [Amazonen. English]
    Amazon parrots: acclimation, care, feeding, illness,
breeding: special chapter, understanding Amazons/
Werner and Susanne Lantermann; translated from the
German by Elizabeth D. Crawford: American advisory
editor, Mathew M. Vriends; with color photographs by
well known animal phtotgraphers and drawings by Fritz
W. Köhler.
    p. cm.
    Translation of: Amazonen.
    Bibliography
    Includes index.
    ISBN 0-8120-4035-X
    1. Amazon parrots. I. Lantermann, Susanne, II.
Vriends, Matthew M., 1937 — . III Title.
SF473.P3L3513 1988
636.6'865 — dc19
                                        88-24061

PRINTED IN HONG KONG
23 22 21 20 19 18 17 16 15 14 13 12

The color photographs on the covers show:
Front cover: Blue-fronted Amazon.
Inside front cover: Blue-fronted Amazon in flight.
Back cover: (above and below left) Blue-fronted Amazons; (below right) Orange-winged Amazon.

Photograph credits:
Angermayer: page 9; Elm: page 10 (below, right); de Grahl: page 10 (above, right); Lantermann: page 47, 48 (below, right), back cover (below, right); Lantermann/ Haase: page 19 (below); Maindok: page 19 (above, right); H. Müller: page 10 (below, right); Reinhard: inside front cover, inside back cover, back cover (above); Scholtz: page 10 (above, left), 48 (above, left and right; below, right); Skogstad: front cover, page 20; Wagner: page 19 (above, left); Wothe: page 37, 38, back cover (below, left).

Werner Lantermann has been director of a private institute for parrot research in Oberhausen since 1981. His special interest centers on the large parrots of Central and South America. He is the author of numerous articles in professional journals and of successful books about parrot-keeping and breeding, among them Barron's *The New Parrot Handbook*.

Susanne Lantermann is Walter Lantermann's co-worker in the private institute for parrot research in Oberhausen and co-author of numerous books about African and South American parrots.

Note and Warning:
People who suffer from allergies to feathers or any kind of feather dust should not keep parrots. In case of doubt, check with the doctor before you acquire one.
In dealing with parrots, one may receive injuries from bites or scratches. Have such wounds attended to by a doctor. Although psittacosis (parrot fever) is not among the commonly seen illnesses of parrots (see page 33), it can produce symptoms in both humans and parrots that may be life-threatening. At any sign of a cold or flu (see page 32), see a doctor immediately.

Contents

Foreword

Wanting an Amazon for a pet is easy to understand, for Amazons — when kept as single birds — rapidly become tame. They usually bond quickly to their keeper, and many of them have a remarkable talent for mimicry. Their striking colors, their engaging ways, and their "high intelligence" fascinate the parrot fancier. But all too often an Amazon is purchased on the spur of the moment. Its future owner knows almost nothing about its life requirements and care needs. Mistakes that have sad consequences for the Amazons as well as their owners are quickly made. How can such mistakes be avoided? The important questions that arise in Amazon keeping are discussed in this book and answered knowledgeably. The authors address not only the keeper of one Amazon but also those who might like to keep a pair or more and even try to breed them.

Parrot experts Werner and Susanne Lantermann have owned and bred Amazons for many years with great success. In this book they pass on their knowledge and experience, telling in detail what you must know about the proper care and maintenance of Amazon parrots. Included is consideration of where you can buy Amazons and what you must watch for when buying. Deciding whether you want to keep your Amazon in a cage, in a room aviary, or in an outdoor flight cage with an aviary will be made easier by the detailed description of the maintenance possibilities. Step by step the authors explain the acclimation and taming of a single bird, and how it learns to "speak"; in addition they tell what exercise Amazons need in order to feel well. The methodical instructions for care, proper nourishment, and feeding will help you to keep your Amazon healthy. But you will also learn to recognize the signs of illness and how to apply emergency measures. Moreover, you will learn how you can avoid such behavior disturbances in a singly kept Amazon as constant screaming or feather picking.

A special chapter is devoted to the eight most popular Amazons now included under the jurisdiction of the species- protection regulations. The description includes facts about appearance, range, and habitat, as well as special advice about maintenance and breeding.

The explanation of Amazon behavior patterns should help you to understand these parrots better. It will also make clear to you why it is both appropriate and desirable to keep Amazons in pairs. Amazons are among the endangered species. To the extent that the captive breeding of Amazons succeeds, the number of the imported wild catch will be decreased. Endeavors to breed to preserve the species therefore take on added importance. Although breeding is not exactly easy, you may dare to attempt it with the help of the authors' detailed introduction to Amazon breeding. This book shows the beginner the way to the proper keeping of Amazons and also offers the experienced Amazon fancier new and useful suggestions.

Authors and publisher thank all who have collaborated on this book: the animal photographers for the extraordinarily beautiful photographs, the artist Fritz W. Köhler for the informative drawings, and the veterinarian Dr. Gabriele Wiesner for checking the chapter on Health Maintenance and Illness.

Before You Get an Amazon

Amazons as Pets

Amazon parrots — usually called Amazons for short — are among the most popular of the large parrots. Their popularity is all too easy to understand, for most parrots — when kept as single birds — allow themselves to be quickly tamed, usually rapidly bond closely to their keeper, and many of them have a pronounced talent for mimicry. In contrast to many others of the large parrots, they get used to living in a cage or an aviary virtually without problems. Also, their appealing ways and their "great intelligence" fascinate the parrot fancier. All these good qualities, which show that the Amazons are adaptable parrots, unfortunately often lead to spur-of-the-moment buying. However, we must urgently warn you against an unconsidered purchase. Only an Amazon that is kept well and properly will develop into a pet that will give you pleasure.

There is also another important reason for not keeping Amazons under inappropriate conditions, one that should furthermore induce you to think of keeping two and raising its young, rather than keeping only one: The survival of many Amazon species in nature is greatly endangered. At this time, 12 of the 27 Amazon species are designated severely endangered or threatened with total extinction by the Washington Endangered Species Convention (Appendix I). All other species are legally regulated by animal protection laws (see page 35).

What to Consider Before Buying

Before you get an Amazon, consider carefully whether you can satisfy its requirements for life. You particularly need to weigh the following points:
• The parrot needs much attention from its caretaker, particularly if it is alone and has no companion.
• It must have freedom of movement — a climbing branch and free flight.
• It needs opportunities to play with things.
• Parrots can live to be very old, and you must care for the bird an entire parrot life.
• Most important of all, if Amazons are going to be kept in a house: Amazons soil things; it can't be avoided.
• Parrots can scream very loudly, which in some circumstances can lead to difficulties with noise-sensitive neighbors — find out ahead of time if the neighbors (and also the landlord!) will tolerate a parrot being kept nearby. The best thing is a written statement.
• Will the Amazon get along with pets you have already (see page 6)?
• People who suffer in any way from feather-dander allergies should not under any circumstances keep parrots. (If in doubt, ask the doctor!)
Note: If you want to keep Amazons in an outdoor aviary — and eventually breed them — you should read about this in the chapter on Breeding Amazons (see page 35).

One Bird or a Pair?

You really should settle this question before you buy, but at least know why it is so important for keeping a parrot.

Social grooming: Two Amazons who get along well with each other groom each other's feathers repeatedly and thoroughly.

Scratching the head is part of grooming behavior. The scratching movements occur so quickly that the eyes can scarcely follow them.

The single bird: The novice parrot keeper will surely begin with a single Amazon. Most likely he or she will try to tame it and teach it to "speak." It is indisputable that for a certain length of time (at least until they become sexually mature) single birds, with constant attention from the keeper, remain in psychological balance and act like ideal house pets. However, with the onset of sexual maturity — about in the fourth or fifth year of life —many single birds exhibit some conspicuous behavioral changes. The parrot is restless; female Amazons frequently lay infertile eggs on the cage floor. Also, the beginnings of feather-picking and other psychological disturbances are noticed at this time.

The pair: Anyone who is closely aquainted with the way of life and the behavior patterns of large parrots will have to admit that in the long run the human as substitute mate cannot fulfill all the social requirements of a parrot. Living together as mates is part of the natural behavior pattern of the Amazon and that of most other large parrots. Even if you cannot decide to get a pair at first, you should not rule out this possibility for sometime in the future. Parrots who get along well together show fascinating behavior in their companionship, which certainly compensates the parrot owner for the fact that the second bird has taken over his role as part-ner. This does not mean at all that once-tamed and "speaking" parrots will turn away from their keeper or become "dumb."

Important: For parrot fanciers who are away from home most of the day and therefore can give little attention to their parrots, keeping a pair is the only thing that can be considered, if indeed parrots should be kept at all.

Children and Amazons

Babies and small children should never be left alone with a parrot without supervision. A parrot can sometimes be very jealous, especially if babies or small children contest their special place in the family. It is possible that they may attack the child and injure it with their sharp claws and powerful beak. After the birth of a baby you must see to it that you do not neglect the Amazon, for in most cases it will soon get used to the newcomer. But, as we have said, never leave the two of them together unsupervised.

Older children and adolescents can gradually become familiar with the habits of an Amazon. They learn with time how to get along properly with the parrot.

Amazons and Other Pets

Dogs and cats: As a rule, Amazons easily get used to a cat or a dog after a short time. Both "parties" learn quickly to accept each other. Basically a large dog or a cat, too, is physically overwhelming to an Amazon, but one should by no means underestimate the defense capabilities of a well-armed parrot. For the first few days it's best if you watch the animals until you are sure that both have come to an agreement or at least will leave each other in peace.

Small mammals: Amazons can be dangerous

Before You Get an Amazon

Warning posture. With raised foot the Amazon threatens his companion, to drive him away from his place.

to hamsters, guinea pigs, mice, or western chipmunks if they actually bite them. Watch how your animals get along with each other; in some cases keeping them in separate rooms is advisable.

Smaller birds: Some Amazons simply ignore smaller birds; but many times the meeting can also be fatal for the smaller bird.

Note: There are no general rules for the way different pets get along together. Close friendships are just as possible as deadly enmity. One must often simply try to find out what works and what doesn't. In any case you should always be alert to be able to intervene and help protect your pets if necessary.

Vacation Care

Before you take a parrot as a pet, it must be clear who is going to take care of the bird while you are on vacation or if you become ill. Most people find a family member or a neighbor who will take over the feeding and the essential care duties. But remember that a single bird also needs attention and conversation during your absence! Often other parrot fanciers in an area will take turns being "vacation stand-in." It's advantageous if Amazons can remain in their familiar surroundings. If necessary you can also take your parrots to the local pet dealer who will take them into his keeping for a fee (find out ahead of time whether he has place and time enough for parrots).

Advice for Buying

Where You Get Amazons

Pet shops: The novice parrot-keeper, especially, should first look around for his new house pet in a well-managed pet store or in the pet department of a large department store. Most of the Amazons sold there are caught in the wild, in their native habitats, and sent on order, by plane, to a wholesaler (a direct importer). There the parrots wait a legally established quarantine period (30 days at this time), during which they undergo psittacosis immunization (see page 56). The quarantine stations are tended and supervised by veterinarians; the birds will be fed a medicated feed as required by the U.S. Public Health Service. After this procedure, which can be very stressful for the parrot, the birds are released to the individual dealers (see page 55) .

Breeders: Many parrot fanciers would like to get their Amazons from a breeder. You must regretfully be told that at this time there are as yet no Amazon breeders. There are dedicated Amazon fanciers who erratically and often purely by accident succeed in raising several young birds, but there can be no talk of breeding in any real sense (see page 35). The total number of Amazon babies born in the U.S.A. and Europe can only be guessed at. The possibility of getting a locally raised Amazon is conceivable, escpecially in states like Florida and California. Sometimes, though, pet dealers and the few "breeders" place advance orders for all the expected broods for the next year. The advantages to having an Amazon born in human captivity are obvious. For one thing, buying the bird does not decimate the natural supply; for another, the Amazon is already well adapted to our climate. Such a parrot is less shy of humans because of its experiences. It is to be hoped that in the future the number of Amazons born in captivity will increase markedly.

Importers: Only someone who has much experience getting parrots used to a new environment should consider buying from a direct importer.

What You Should Watch For When Buying

Give yourself lots of time to buy your Amazon. Make certain first that the living quarters of the parrots you are offered are clean and that the food supply is properly arranged. In addition, you should look carefully at the Amazons. It is certainly not at all easy to judge the health condition of an Amazon, but some essential points to look for can help you to come to a fairly certain judgment.

Behavior: Observe the parrot you are interested in from a distance for a while. It should be lively (naturally, the frequent rest periods are the exception), occasionally climbing around in the cage; no forced movements should be visible; while resting crouching on one foot or while eating, it should be able to take large pieces of food in one claw while sitting on the other without wavering and with no loss of balance.

Appearance: Now observe the parrot close up. Its eyes should be clear and shining, the nostrils dry and clear, the area around the nose also dry and not stuck with little pieces of feather. If this is not the case, you should avoid buying it. Also not recommended is the purchase of an Amazon on whom you can discern external wounds or beak irregularities (broken pieces of beak, anomalies of position of upper and lower mandible). Missing toes, toe segments, or claws are beauty flaws that, except for drastic examples, should not force you to give up the idea of buying.

A shining, smooth, colorful plumage suggests that the Amazon is healthy. But almost all newly imported parrots have a dull and to some degree imperfect and rumpled plumage, as a result of capture and transport — without being sick.

Two Amazons that get along well together. Left in the picture a subspecies of the red-lored Amazon (*Amazona autumnalis salvini* or Salvin's Amazon); right, orange-winged Amazon (*Amazona amazonica*).

Feces: In a healthy parrot the droppings consist of a partly olive-green and a partly white urine portion of medium-firm consistency. Deviations from this in color, and also watery droppings can indicate an illness of the intestinal tract. However, food changes and unusual experiences (stress, for example) can produce symptoms of diarrhea in a parrot for a short time without its being actually sick (see page 32).

The nutritional condition: Ask the seller to catch the parrot you have chosen so that you can check how well nourished the bird is. Carefully feel the breast musculature with your hand: fleshy muscle webs on both sides of the readily palpable ridge of the breastbone indicate a well-nourished parrot. Individual muscle parts with a sharply prominent breastbone are typical of a starving bird. Inexperienced parrot keepers should not buy such a one.

The wings: If you hold the Amazon in your hand, it is easy to check the integrity of the pinions to see the degree of cutting of the wing feathers, which has usually been done in the country of origin. Pay particular attention to the outside joint (third finger of the middle hand bone). Occasionally, with too drastic cutting methods, it is affected, so that the feathers will no longer grow in this place and the parrot can no longer fly.

Age Determination

The exact age of an Amazon cannot be established except in the case of the captive-bred bird.

Popular Amazon species.
Above left: green-cheeked or red-crowned Amazon (*Amazona viridigenalis*); above right: a subspecies of the yellow-crowned Amazon, the *Amazona ochrocephala panamensis* or Panama yellow-headed Amazon); below left: lilac-crowned Amazon (*Amazona finschi*); below right: mealy Amazon (*Amazona farinosa*).

With a newly imported parrot you can begin with the idea that it must be at least six months old, if you consider the nestling period and add in the time spent in the camp of the South American trapper and in quarantine. If you are dealing with a retail store you must also reckon in the time the parrot has spent there. But it is possible that the parrot is substantially older, for adult parrots are also captured and brought into trade.

Characteristics of a Young Bird

Signs of a young bird are a dirty gray-brown iris, subdued plumage color, less strongly defined color characteristics compared to old birds, fine horny scales on the feet, and a smooth beak without horny

Stretching. After a rest or sleeping phase the parrot stretches.

stratifications. On the whole, young birds are smaller and lighter than grown animals.

In all Amazons the iris color undergoes a change and within two to three years—at least in the species well known up to now—reaches its final red, red-orange, or chestnut-brown color. Color markings and intensity of plumage color are not completely defined until five years of age. For the person inexperienced with parrots, the difference between young and old birds is scarcely noticeable.

Advice for Buying

Sex Determination

With two exceptions, Amazon males and females are not distinguishable from one another by any external features. Most of the external marks that are vigorously discussed in the parrot literature and among parrot experts are much too uncertain to be relied on.

For the keeper of a single bird it is unimportant what sex his Amazon is, since males as well as females have the same "aptitude" for becoming good house pets.

Endoscopy

On the other hand, for the breeder it is important to determine the sex of his birds to avoid years of failed breeding attempts. Leparoscopy (endoscopy of the abdominal cavity) has so far shown itself to be a relatively low-risk method. For a fee it can be done by many veterinarians and bird clinics with nearly 100 percent success. The Amazon must be anesthetized; a small incision under the bottom rib permits passage of an endoscope (a tiny mirror with a lighting apparatus), with which the sex organs can be visualized directly. As a rule there are no complications of any sort from the anesthetic and after awakening the bird is quickly back to sitting on its perch.

Important: Debilitated, sick, and quarantined birds should not undergo endoscopy.

Amazon Species with External Sex Characteristics

Two Amazon species, the yellow-lored Amazon (*Amazona xantholora*) and the white-fronted Amazon (*Amazona albifrons*), allow distinction between the sexes because of their plumage color. The yellow-lored Amazon is rarely seen in trade, so for the majority of parrot-keepers only the differential markings of the white-fronted Amazon are of any importance. Male white-fronted Amazons have red at the front edge of the wing and a red wing speculum, whereas the females as a rule are pure green in this area.

Nevertheless, young females with individual red feathers at the wing front are occasionally described in the literature.

Buying Formalities

When you buy the Amazon you have carefully chosen and observed, there are still some formalities to undergo.

• In Europe the Amazon is required to wear an official leg band with a number, which the seller must note in his records together with your address.

Sleeping posture. Healthy parrots sleep on one leg; the other leg is pulled into the belly feathers; the head is turned 180 degrees to the rear and tucked into the back feathers.

• In a European pet store, as a matter of course, you will receive a proper bill on which the ring number is also noted. If you buy in another place, be sure to ask the seller for a bill that contains the name and address of the seller and buyer, the sale price, and the ring number.
• In the U.S. ask for a CITES certificate; today for any animal listed in the Washington Endangered Species Convention (Appendices I and II) this certificate can be provided by an animal dealer if

the animal is legally imported.

• If, according to the pet dealer, a sex determination of the Amazon has already been made, demand a written confirmation.

• The species protection regulations in force at the time of the sale must be observed, and in a good pet store this will always be the case. In other situations it is advisable to be informed about the regulations before you buy (see Washington Endangered Species Convention, page 35 and Bringing Birds into the USA, page 55).

Two Serious Threats to Birds

As a bird owner, you should know the symptoms of exotic *Newcastle disease*, the devastating disease of poultry and other birds. If your birds show signs of incoordination and breathing diffi-

culties — or if there should be any unusual die-off among them — contact your local veterinarian or animal health official immediately. Place dead birds in plastic bags, and refrigerate them for submittal to a diagnostic laboratory. Keep in mind that this disease is highly contagious, and you should isolate any newly purchased birds for at least 30 days. Although exotic Newcastle disease is not a general health hazard, it can cause minor eye infections in humans.

If you're tempted to buy a bird you suspect may have been smuggled into the United States, don't! Smuggled birds are a persistent threat to the health of birds and poultry flocks in this country. Indications are that many recent outbreaks of exotic Newcastle disease were caused by birds entering the United States illegally. If you have information about the possibility of smuggled birds, report it to any U.S. Customs office or call APHIS at Hyattsville, Maryland, (301) 436-8061.

For the keeper of a single bird it is unimportant what sex his Amazon is, since males as well as females have the same "aptitude" for becoming good house pets.

Housing

The Cage

The majority of Amazons are kept in a cage in the home. Their cage must not become a constricting prison, so you should only buy a cage in which they will be able to feel comfortable.

The Cage Size: The parrot cages that are generally available, with dimensions of 16 x 16 x 23 inches (40 x 40 x 60 cm) or 16 x 16 x 31 inches (40 x 40 x 80 cm), are much too small for keeping even

A well-equipped parrot cage . Two Amazons can live in a cage like this if they have opportunities to fly regularly.

a single parrot. These cages may be useful during the brief acclimation period or for caring for an ailing Amazon, but there is no question of their being a permanent accommodation. To provide for the Amazon's need for movement you should choose one of the cages that is offered as an indoor aviary in pet stores and in the pet departments of the larger department stores. They are 39 to 59 inches (100-150 cm) high and have a floor surface of about 23 x 39 inches (60 x 100 cm). There is a whole line of models, so you can certainly find an appropriate Amazon cage that will fit in with your decor (if that is important to you).

Cage Shape: A parrot cage should have a rectangular or square bottom; round cages are unsuitable.

The Cage Mesh: Since Amazons like to climb, the cage bars should be horizontal on at least two sides of the cage. The spaces between the bars should be at least 0.6 inches (15 mm) wide and at most 1 inch (25 mm), and the bars should be thick enough so that even a large Amazon can't bend or bite through them.

Floor surface: A pan for catching droppings that can be pulled out of the bottom like a drawer makes the work of regular cleaning much easier. In some cages a wire grate is fastened about an inch (a few centimeters) above the floor, which is supposed to keep the Amazons away from their excrement and the food droppings in order to decrease the risk of illness. However, this floor grating keeps the birds from being able to pick up small stones from the sand litter, and these stones promote their digestion. If you don't want to remove the grill, it's essential that you provide a good bird sand or grit in a separate food dish. Failure to get these essential little stones or a proper parrot grit over a protracted period of time can have serious consequences for the Amazon and may even result in its death.

Cage door: It must be large enough so that you can reach into the cage easily, and the bird can climb in and out without any difficulty.

Room Aviaries

Room aviaries with a height of at least 70 inches (180 cm) and a floor of at least 39 x 59 inches (100 x 150 cm) are recommended for Amazons. An accommodation of this size is suitable for both a single bird and a pair of Amazons.

Fasten a nest box firmly to the back wall, which usually consists of a solid piece of wood.

The available cages range from ready-made room-sized aviaries to components and mesh of various different measurements. It's best to take the advice of the pet dealer; he will show you the manufacturer's catalogs and help you with the choice of a suitable cage. Parrot keepers who are handy can of course expend some effort and build their own large room aviary of galvanized square mesh 0.6 x 0.6 inches (15 x 15 mm) or stronger; see also Outdoor Shelter and Flight Cage, page 16.

Fittings for Cages and Room Aviaries

Perches: The perches should be of wood (beech), should be either round or square with rounded edges, and should be 1 to 1-1/2 inches (25 to 35 mm) thick. Highly recommended are various-sized branches of fruit trees that have not been sprayed (in any case, be sure to take the precaution of scrubbing with hot water). These are good because their rough surface will wear down the claws of the Amazon naturally so they won't have to be cut. Besides, different sizes of branches offer the parrots a kind of "foot exercise" that helps to prevent laming of their feet.

Food and Drinking Containers: Standard plastic or pottery dishes are usually included in the price of a cage; you can get replacements or other dishes (there should be four, see page 29) in the pet store. Plastic dishes should be changed after about two years, because by that time they can no longer be cleaned thoroughly. Don't place food and drink-ing dishes under the perches where they can be fouled by falling droppings. Mount dishes that stand on a feeding shelf — often the case in large aviaries —so that the parrots can't knock them to the floor. The stainless-steel feed and water dishes in a special holder (available in the pet store) are very practical for cages and aviaries.

Playthings: Climbing ropes, chains with large links, fresh branches for gnawing, clean stones that the birds can take in their beaks but can't swallow, and parrot playthings of wood, available in the pet store, supply the single bird and also the aviary birds with variety and chances for play.

Placement of Cages and Room Aviaries: A parrot home should not be constantly moved back and forth, should be in a place protected from drafts, and should not be exposed to cigarette smoke or cooking odors.

A quiet corner in the living room that is bright, airy, draft-free, and occasionally sunny is appropriate. Never put the cage in the middle of the room; without the backing of a wall or a corner, the birds feel insecure.

The cage must not stand on the floor. Amazons feel most comfortable and secure if they view their surroundings from a somewhat elevated lookout such as eye level.

You should always have the cage of a single bird in the most used room so that the parrot can take part in family life and not be bored.

Free-standing Perch and Climbing Tree

Acclimated, hand-tame Amazons can be kept for hours, even in some cases constantly, on a perch or climbing tree outside the cage. It's a welcome change for the Amazon, and the parrot owner can maintain good contact with his bird and enjoy watching its acrobatics.

Free-standing perches are available ready-made at the pet store. Hobbyists who want to offer their parrot more than the commercially available smooth round rod can make the free-standing perch even more varied by means of natural branches (see drawing at the right).

For a climbing tree you need a forked piece of branch or a small tree as well as a sand-filled container such as a cement or wooden planter. Branch sections or tree must be firmly fastened in the container with metal corners.

Keeping the Amazon on a climbing tree or a free-standing perch is very much to be recommended, but as a rule you have to supervise the bird. Amazons that are able to fly will gladly undertake expeditions through the house or apartment and can do damage or be injured themselves. Amazons whose wings have been clipped on one side very seldom leave the free-standing perch or the climbing tree voluntarily, probably because in the beginning they experienced, often painfully, what happened when they tried to fly with only one wing intact.

For an outdoor climbing tree, fruit trees are

Free-standing parrot perch: A perch bought in a pet store can be made to offer much variety with the addition of natural branches.

eminently suitable. The tree must be shortened to a height that you can see over. However, fruit trees that you want to keep should not be subjected to the beaks of Amazons. Keeping the bird outside can only be considered in good weather, with wing-clipped Amazons, and under supervision, for Amazons can fall from trees or climb down and subsequently "run away" or else become the victims of lurking cats or the neighbors' dogs.

Outdoor Shelter and Flight Cage

If you want to keep parrots, and perhaps even breed them, we recommend the setup of an outdoor aviary with an attached flight cage. In the literature (see page 58) you will find books that tell you how to build this kind of an enclosure, or you can commission one from a local building firm .

Tips for Building the Bird Shelter

To make your planning easier, there are some basic things you need to consider when building an aviary:

• Find out about local building regulations and whether a building permit is necessary.

• In our experience an aviary with stone walls is best suited for keeping parrots (wood has some drawbacks—for instance, because of the "gnawing fever" of many Amazons).

• The shelter needs a cement foundation.

• Don't forget to plan for windows (preferably of glass brick) and doors (inquire about door dimensions ahead of time).

• The roof is best made of glass brick or wood. Tar paper does well to make the roof watertight.

• For Amazon parrots the house must be slightly heated in winter; to cut down on the cost of heating, insulation is recommended.

• The fly-through to the flight cage is created by swivel-mounted glass-brick windows or tin sliding panels.

Housing

• Furnishing the shelter with fluorescent light, several humidity-proof wall sockets, a heat source, and running water attached to a drain is highly recommended.
• The size of the protected area: A ground surface of 39 x 39 inches (1 m x 1 m) and a height of 59 to 79 inches (1.5-2 m) is enough for an Amazon pair; the space should be no smaller than this.
• The equipment of the interior room consists of a feeding shelf with inset dishes, several perches, and a nesting box.

The Open Flight Cage

The flight cage is attached to the shelter, so that in periods of bad weather or in winter the parrots can seek their inner room without hindrance. Brief information about building a flight cage follows:
• It is advisable to lay a cement foundation — about 23 to 31 inches (60-80 cm) deep to keep out rats and other uninvited "guests."
• For Amazons a length of 79 to 118 inches (2-3

meters) is sufficient; the width is determined by the width of the shelter.
• Welded, galvanized steel pipes are best to use for the framework of the flight cage.
• A part of the flight cage will be roofed with galvanized tin or plastic sheets, the remainder covered with wire fencing (galvanized rectangular mesh, mesh width 0.5 x 1 inch [12.5 x 25 mm], 0.7 x 0.7 inch [17.5 x 17.5 mm], or 1 x 1 inch [25 x 25 mm], wire gauge at least 0.04 inch [1 mm]).
• We recommend paving stones as flooring. A solid cement floor leads to pooling of water during extended rainy spells; and within a short time floors of natural ground are so full of pathogens that hygienic parrot maintenance can no longer be guaranteed.
• At least two perches should be installed in a flight cage — depending on its size — and placed as far away — from each other as possible to leave room for flying; there should also be a branched climbing and gnawing tree and a bird bath as well.

Acclimation and Care

Taking the Amazon Home

A newly acquired Amazon should be transported to its future home as quickly as possible. Wooden boxes or firm cardboard cartons with dimensions of about 10 x 10 x 18 inches (25 x 25 x 45 cm) are good carrying containers.

For short journeys a cardboard carton will do; it must have airholes punched in it.

For longer trips you need a stable carrier, which should contain a perch and a filled food dish. Special animal-carrying crates with a wire-covered opening for ventilation are ideal; these are available in a pet store or you can build the carrier yourself.

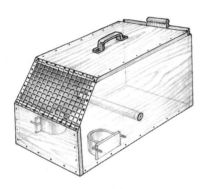

Parrot transport box for the do-it-yourself builder. You need 1/2 inch- (10-15-mm-) thick plywood and narrow-mesh wire caging. The box will close at the back by means of a drop panel or a trap.

It is important that the traveling cage be closed—except for the wire-covered ventilation hole—so that the bird does not become terrified by the constantly changing impressions during a journey by bus, train, or car and begin to flutter around wildly in the carrier. Cages are not suitable for transporting parrots for this reason. The bird can injure itself badly by flapping around.

Acclimation

Once arrived home, release the parrot from its traveling carrier into the cage that is standing ready, in which the food dishes are already filled and the floor is covered with sand. Open the carrier and hold the opening in front of the cage door in such a way that the parrot cannot escape. If it still manages to escape, whatever you do avoid going on a "wild chase" after the new arrival, who is still doubtless frightened from the journey. You will only succeed in getting the anxious fugitive into its new house with calm, patience, and perhaps some unusual delicacy. Leave your Amazon completely at peace for the first few days. Only make sure it takes enough food. In the beginning offer the bird familiar food (ask when you buy it) and only later slowly correct the nutritional palette (see Feeding, page 27).

Note: Also put aviary birds in a cage to get acclimated at first; never put them with other birds immediately, either with those of their own species or with others.

First Fecal Examination: After the Amazon has lived alone for several days and has become calmer, and its feces have gone from nervously induced diarrhea to a normal, firm consistency, take a fecal sample. In the evening a plastic sheet is spread under the perch; this is removed the next morning with the droppings, and immediately the fecal sample is placed in a clean glass jar and taken to the veterinarian for examination. If any treatment is necessary, you must follow the advice of the veterinarian exactly.

Amazon young.
Above left: Yellow-crowned Amazon (8 weeks old); above right: Yellow-cheeked Amazon (6 weeks old); below: Salvin's Amazons (8 weeks old).

Placement in an Aviary

A newcomer may be placed in an already occupied cage only when the first fecal examination shows it to be free of infection or when any necessary treatment is successfully concluded. This is necessary to protect the older inhabitants of the aviary from contagious illness. Furthermore the bird must be completely healthy, because now a period of further stress is beginning for it as it experiences change and gets used to its new surroundings. It must become familiar with new relationships, with partner birds or rivals, and must if necessary fight for its ranking and access to the food dish. In any case you must devote special attention to it in the first months—just as for a single bird—in order to be able to intervene as quickly as possible at the first signs of indisposition.

Advice for Making Your Parrot Hand-Tame

An Amazon becomes accustomed the most rapidly of all the parrot species to the presence of human beings and will usually quickly become quiet and comfortable in the cage. The acclimation phase and the period just after it, when the parrot spends its time exclusively in the cage, are most opportune for beginning hand-taming. But give the parrot a few days time at first to get used to its new surrounding. Besides it should already recognize your voice and know that you threaten no danger. These are important prerequisites for hand-taming.

White-fronted Amazon (*Amazona albifrons*) with a piece of apple in its claw.

The First Step in Taming: When the Amazon no longer withdraws from you and now watches its human companions with interest, it is not long until it will take the first treat out of your hand. To begin with, put the treat into the cage. You must move cautiously and quietly so that the bird does not become frightened and peck at your hand with its beak. In time the hand that offers the treat will become less and less feared, and at some point the time will come when you can playfully scratch your Amazon for the first time without its recoiling or even biting. After several weeks — but it can also take longer with some parrots — the Amazon has accepted the hand as the substitute for the social plumage care that parrots otherwise carry out for each other and sooner or later will hold its head next to the cage wire with its neck feathers lightly spread out as an invitation for scratching.

The second step in hand-taming is more difficult. For now your parrot has to get used to getting onto your hand. Quietly hold one hand out to it and with the other offer it a treat, which you slowly pull back so that the bird is forced to put one foot on the outstretched hand. Only with endless patience and regular repetition will this finally succeed in moving the parrot to climb onto the extended hand. Stay calm and keep from doing anything that might frighten the Amazon. Even if it pecks your hand or tries to bite you, be patient and bear in mind constantly: You can't train a parrot like a dog. Punishment in any form is meaningless and destroys the carefully built-up relationship of trust.

How Amazons Learn to "Speak"

It's time to think of "speech training" only when the Amazon has largely gotten over its shyness. Because the bird is at its most receptive in the evening hours, the training should be done every evening. Parrots learn most quickly words that contain many vowels (a,e,i,o,u). The training program thus begins with words like Mama, Papa,

Acclimation and Care

Grandma, or Hello. Sibilants are the hardest sounds for a parrot to learn. Through frequent talking in front of it and regular repetition almost every Amazon will learn some words. Some parrots — depending on disposition and capability — develop into regular "performers" who can repeat whole sentences or many words; others are talented whistlers, whistling melodies — even in different pitches. Still others are able to reproduce sounds that they frequently hear in their environment.

The mimicking of Amazons — in contrast to the performance of an African Gray parrot — usually sounds quite parrotlike, in part even meaningless and many times only suggesting the tone in which one has spoken words or sentences to it or tones that they have heard most frequently.

Please do not expect too much of your Amazon; not every Amazon is a "performer," but almost every one does — with proper care and maintenance — develop into a lovable, devoted house pet.

Why Parrots Can "Speak"

Parrots belong to the mockers in the bird world, that is to those birds who are able to imitate sounds.

For eating the Amazon uses its foot like a hand to hold bits of food firmly.

Among them only parrots have developed the ability to a true mastery. Still, every "speech utterance" of a parrot is merely a mechanical repetition, for it doesn't understand the meaning of its words. Of course many parrots can connect certain circumstances meaningfully with one another and so it often has the appearance of repeating some words with understanding and at the right moment.

When you want to teach a parrot "speech" or imitation, you develop and use his natural ability. But nevertheless this is not behavior that could hitherto have been established in nature, although it is assumed that parrots imitated sounds frequently heard there, such as the voices of other animals.

Play and Activities

Singly kept parrots need regular activity to make their solitude bearable. Parrots who live in aviaries are less subject to the danger that they will vegetate and pine away from boredom because they have roomier living quarters, branching perches, and climbing trees, as well as companions and brooding activities. On the other hand, this danger is a constant one for the single parrot. If an Amazon is left alone too much, if it has neither a companion nor a human substitute partner around it regularly, changes occur in the bird. At first the Amazon becomes completely quiet, sits all day, hour after hour, in the same spot on its perch and leaves it only occasionally for feeding. Frequently such poor creatures turn to constant screeching and pulling out their feathers; some even begin to mutilate themselves (see feather eating, feather picking, page 33). You must avoid the possibility of these negative developments by providing varied activities or, even better, by getting your Amazon a partner.

"Playthings" for Amazons
Offer your Amazon variety and occupation by furnishing the birdcage (and, of course, the aviary

and the flight cages, too) with large-linked chains and ropes for gnawing and climbing, with fresh branches, and with "toys" tumbling on chains (for instance of wood or of unprinted cardboard). There are almost no limits on your inventiveness. The more varied the opportunities for activity are, the better. It's important to use material that isn't harmful to the bird or can't be bitten (some plastic toys) and swallowed. But remember, providing all these chances for activity doesn't exempt you from the attention that you must give your single Amazon daily and in sufficient quantity!

During a shower bath the parrot turns and bends and spreads its wings wide, so that the stream of water can reach all over its feathers.

Flying Free in the House

Free flight inside the house is necessary for two reasons: First, to provide the bird with some change, and second, to offer it adequate opportunities for exercise. As soon as your parrot has gotten over its shyness, you should open the cage door and accustom it an hour at a time to being outside the cage. It's best if you place the bird on a climbing tree. If you furnish it with some fresh branches, the Amazon will soon adopt it as its favorite place—and will lose interest in such landing spots as lampshades or cupboard edges.

Let the parrot fly and climb around the room only under supervision, since it can injure itself in some situations (see Table of Dangers, page 26) or else can damage the furniture with its sharp beak. The parrot should always find its food in the cage, then it will quickly learn to clamber back there when it gets hungry. It should always spend the night in the cage.

Care of the Amazon

The "Shower Bath"

A weekly shower helps parrots to keep their plumage in order.

In the house parrots are best showered with a hand-held water sprayer. Use only lukewarm water and provide a gentle water stream (use a fine mist and not a stream of water. All parrots are skeptical about such showering at the beginning; therefore you must get them used to it slowly and carefully until they are comfortable with the weekly showering procedure. Do not use a mister/sprayer that has previously contained household cleaning solutions.

In the flight cage in summer a warm rain shower can take the place of the shower, or the inmates can be sprayed weekly with a hose to which a fine spray head has been attached.

The showering time is morning, preferably, so that the parrots are stimulated to a careful preening of the damp feathers and can be dry again before dark.

All parrots learn to enjoy the weekly shower; some birds may even enjoy it daily!

Cutting Claws

Rough perching branches of different sizes normally hamper overgrowth of claws. Should the claws become too long nevertheless, they must be cut. You can hold a tame parrot in your hand for this, grasping his toes between two fingers. A parrot that is not tame must be caught (wear leather

Acclimation and Care

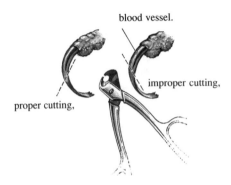

Cutting claws: Left, correctly done; right, incorrectly done. The blood vessel must not be injured!

gloves!) and held firmly with both hands, while a helper cuts the claws.

Cutting Claws Properly: Using a sharp pair of nail clippers, cut the claws to normal length (see drawing). Be careful not to injure the blood vessel. In Amazon species that have bright, horn-colored claws, it's easy to see the blood vessel if you hold the claw against a bright light source. In Amazons with dark claws, claw cutting should be undertaken only with extreme caution.

If, in spite of all care, bleeding occurs because the claws were cut too short, put the bird back in the cage and let it stay there completely undisturbed for a while. The bleeding will usually come to a stop by itself; if this is not the case, you should call a veterinarian for advice.

Important note: Inexperienced parrot-keepers should have the claw cutting done by a veterinarian or a pet dealer.

Shortening the Beak

Abnormally long beak growth and particularly the occasional deformities that occur in the beak area (such as "crooked bite") are not always caused by lack of opportunity to wear it down. Sometimes the cause is a metabolic disturbance resulting from inadequate diet. You should never, under any

circumstances, undertake correction of beak abnormalities yourself, but always leave them to an experienced veterinarian!

Care of the Cage

A parrot cage must be cleaned regularly; a dirty cage can cause disease. The following cleaning procedures are necessary.

Wing clipping. Trim the secondaries and the inner primaries (the white part of the feathers) on both wings. Never clip just one wing only! The Amazon would lose its balance when trying to take off and would fall to the ground.

Daily: Clean feed and water dishes, refill, empty spoiled food remains out of the floor tray.

Weekly: Empty the dropping tray and clean, dry, and spread the floor with a thin layer of clean sand. Use clean beach sand or the "bird sand" you can buy in a pet store, which has the advantage of an anise additive, which helps to keep down the odors around the birdcage.

Caution: Do not spread the cage floor with newspaper or, especially, aluminum foil! It's dangerous for the parrot if it eats any of it. And besides, it then can't eat the stones that foster digestion (see page 28), which are contained in sand.

Every Six Months: In galvanized or chrome-plated cages scrub the perches and the cage mesh thoroughly under hot running water. Wash brass cages with lukewarm water and dry with a towel.

As Necessary: Replace plastic dishes with new ones, since they become unsightly with time and then can no longer be thoroughly cleaned.

Cleaning of Aviary and Flight Cage

Daily: Clean feed and water dishes, refill, and remove spoiled food remains.

Weekly: (or every 2 weeks): Rake out the floor of the cage and, whenever necessary, spread with clean sand.

Yearly: General cleaning is best done in fall, after the breeding season. With the help of a garden hose and a scrub brush clean the bird shelter and the cage thoroughly and afterwards disinfect it; replace perches, renew the sand on the floor.

Important: All parrots must be removed to another place during the cleaning and may only be returned to the aviary when the house is dry, the remains of the disinfectant have dried away, and the cage floor has been spread with new sand.

Table of Dangers

Souce of Danger	Consequences	How to Avoid
Bathroom	Flying out of an open window. Drowning by falling into open toilet or filled sink or tub. Poisoning by cleaning materials, etc.	Keep parrots out of the bathroom; never leave the bathroom door open.
Electric wires	Shock from gnawing or biting through wires.	Conceal wires under moldings and carpets, behind cupboards, or unplug.
Poisons	Severe disturbances (gastro-intestinal, neurals, etc.) by tin, copper, nicotine, mercury, plastic-coated bowls, cleaning materials and insecticides; harmful are pencil lead, ballpoint and felt-tip pens, alcohol, coffee, spices.	Remove any and all poisonous lethal materials from the bird's surroundings, or at least prevent it from getting at them. Be especially careful about lead curtain weights — parrots love to gnaw on them.
Poisonous trees, bushes, houseplants	Severe disturbances, often fatal.	Don't give bird any branches of poisonous trees or bushes to chew on. For example, the following are poisonous: acacia, birch, yew, laburnum, viburnun, holly, dwarf elder, and all conifers. Keep the parrots from nibling or eating houseplants.
Plate glass	Flying into it, resulting in concussion or broken neck.	Cover glass (windows, balcony doors, glass walls) with curtains or get the parrot used to what is for him an invisible room boundary: lower shades to two-thirds; increase the uncovered surface a bit each day.
Adhesives	Poisoning with fatal outcome caused by volatile solvents.	Remove all animals from the room while using adhesives and air the room very thoroughly after work is finished.
Kitchen	Steam and fumes burden the respiratory passages; overheated kitchens and necessary ventilation lead to colds and other illnesses. Burns from stove burners, turned off but still hot, and from hot food in open containers.	Don't keep birds in the kitchen or else air it regularly — be careful, however that there are no drafts. Place pots of water on hot burners that are not in use; cover pots.
Doors	Caught or crushed in carelessly closed or opened door. Birds may also fly away.	Accidents and escape can only be avoided with the greatest vigilance.
Cigarettes	Smoky air is injurious; nicotine is fatal.	It's best not to smoke in the vicinity of the bird, but at least ventilate regularly (avoid drafts!).
Drafts	Cold, lung inflammations.	Avoid drafts no matter what!

Proper Diet

According to existing information from the wild, Amazons are unspecialized seed and fruit eaters, and therefore in captivity they quickly get used to a substitute feed.

The Basic Diet

The parrot feed offered in the pet stores (in combination with the additional supplements discussed below!) is generally regarded as suitable for Amazons. It consists of 40 to 50 percent white, striped and/or black sunflower seeds, with the other 50 to 60 percent divided among equal parts of peanuts, corn, oats, wheat, rice, millet and canary grass seed or white seed and thistle. Pinetree seeds and pumpkin seeds are sometimes also ingredients in this mixture. However, we have some doubts as to whether the high fat content of the sunflower seeds (54 percent), which often make up the major portion of the mixture, is particularly beneficial to the digestive tract of the Amazon; furthermore, sunflower seeds lack lysine (important for feather growth) and are very addictive due to their sweet taste. Therefore we assemble the feed mixture for our parrots ourselves — you can get all the ingredients at the pet store or from a feed dealer or buy one of the better-known commercial brands. The proportions of the mixture are about 30 percent sunflower seeds, 35 percent thistle as well as 35 percent of other seeds like millet, sorghum, rice, wild rice, buckwheat, white seed, and oats. Acorns, hazelnuts, walnuts, and pine nuts are considered treats by many Amazons. All the same, we only give our Amazons very small amounts of them.

Sprouted Feed

Seed sprouts are enjoyed by many Amazons—once they get used to it. This sprouted feed is important for a healthy diet for Amazons, especially in winter when there is no green food and fruit is expensive, but also shortly before and during reproduction. In the stores there are contrivances (so-called sprouting boxes) that make the production of sprouts much easier. Appropriate seeds are oats, wheat, and also small seeds, such as those sold for small parakeets, canaries, and waxbills. All seeds are separated from one another and sprouted and then combined in one dish at feeding.

The simplest method for production of sprouted feed: Put two days' supply of seed in a dish, cover the seeds with water, and place in a warm spot. After 24 hours shake the seeds, which will have swollen, in a fine-meshed sieve and wash them thoroughly under running water. Then spread the seeds on flat wire racks, keep them warm, and during the next 24 hours rinse them thoroughly several times. After two or three days, depending on the action of the warmth, the sprouts will have broken through on the oats and wheat. Wash again and offer to the parrots in a separate dish. Give the parrots only as much as they can eat in a few hours.

Important: In summer the dish must be removed after a few hours and cleaned, because sprouted feed rots quickly in warm temperatures.

Fruit and Green Feed

In the wild, parrots gain a large part of their nutritional requirements by eating various kinds of fruit and fresh greenery. Appropriate food—that is, fruit and greenery—should also be included in the diet of a parrot in captivity.

Fruit: After becoming acclimated, parrots eat everything that the store or your own garden has to offer: apples, pears, plums, cherries, grapes, also exotic fruits like oranges, bananas, mangos, papayas, kiwis, and whatever other fruit there is. Added to that are carrots, cucumbers, pieces of pumpkin and zucchini, berries of all kinds (strawberries, cranberries, blueberries, gooseberries, red currants) as well as the red fruits of the mountain ash, and the hips of the dog rose (Rosa canina).

Green Feed: The palette of the suitable green feeds ranges from garden vegetables (lettuce, spinach, white beet, dandelion leaves) to the countless wild plants like shepherd's purse and chickweed.

Important: If you want to collect wild plants yourself, learn about them in the literature (see page 58). Collect only those plants that you can identify without any doubt.

Caution: Chickweed is easy to confuse with the poisonous spurge. Definite identifying characteristic: If you break the stem of spurge, it exudes a milky fluid, whereas chickweed does not.

Suitable food plants. Left, dandelion; right, flower stem and a whole plant of shepherd's purse; above right, chickweed.

Animal Feed

Although parrots prefer to eat plants and their seeds and fruits, they also need animal protein. This need can be met with small portions of hard-boiled egg, cottage cheese, cheese, or canned dog food — given regularly, at ten-day intervals.

Inappropriate Food for Parrots

Strongly seasoned food from the family table is very unhealthy for parrots. Even if your Amazon begs and is agitating for a slice of sausage or casts sidelong glances at a mouthful of stew, such things do not belong in the parrot's diet.

Breeding Food

Circumstances permitting, you should give an Amazon pair that is ready to breed a special breeding food (see Amazon breeding, page 39). The pair will already be used to the food before the birth of the young, so that there will be no slowdown in the food supply after the the babies are born.

The breeding food is made of an egg mixture (available from the pet store) and grated carrots (the mixture should be damp and crumbly). As necessary, they can also be given vitamins, calcium, fruit, and small pieces of cut-up egg, and greenery. To accustom the Amazons quickly to the unusual but very nutritious feed, offer it many times in succession.

Vitamins and Minerals

The diet described is complete and sufficient. All the same, in winter, when there is little fruit and little greenery around to feed, or after vacation, when the "substitute" has fed the parrot only with the basics, we recommend adding a multivitamin preparation to the drinking water, to avoid the development of any deficiencies (dosage and application according to the manufacturer's instructions).

Amazons can get the necessary minerals with calcium available from the pet store, which you sprinkle over fruit and sprouts or mix in with the breeding food weekly. In addition Amazons need grit or ordinary river sand; this also serves to supply their mineral requirements and besides, the grinding function assists the gizzard. These food additives are necessary for life; if they are lacking for a long period of time the parrot can even die because it can't digest its food properly. Therefore, you should always use sand on the bottom of the cage and offer grit in a separate dish.

Drinking Water

Amazons need fresh tap water daily. In districts with bad drinking water, treat the water with a filter or use spring water, available in gallon containers at your grocery store.

Don't put the water dish near the food dish, for almost all Amazons are very wasteful of their food and spread it around the whole cage. The food remnants will dirty the water even sooner than usual.

Proper Feeding.

To permit proper feeding of the parrot in calibrated amounts, the cage should contain four dishes: one dish each for mixed seeds and clean drinking water, one for finely chopped green feed, fruit, sprouts (alternating) or when necessary, breeding food, and the fourth dish should always contain sand or grit. Be sure that the dishes are always clean, and give each parrot or pair the same dishes in the usual arrangement.

Feeding Time: Always feed at the same time, either in the morning or the afternoon. We always feed our Amazons between four and five o'clock, a bit earlier in winter. They are very active at this time and furthermore they can ingest enough food before nightfall.

Quantities: The feed you put out should always consist half of dried seeds and half of green feed, fruit, and sprouts. Before and during the breeding period the portion of sprouted seed can be increased and the ordinary diet can be enriched with breeding food. The daily amount is determined by the activity of the parrot. Caged birds, who move little, need about 2.8 ounces (80 grams) of seeds per day and about the same quantity of fruit. This accords with the size of the feed dish that is usually supplied with the commercially available parrot cage.

Amazons kept in a small inside aviary in winter need, per pair and day, about 6.3 ounces (180 grams) of seed and the same amount of fruit. During the flight-cage season (during the warm season) this quantity increases to about 8.75 ounces (250 grams) of seed and the same amount of fruit (and for reproduction, many times more).

Health and Illness

With proper maintenance and good care Amazons seldom become sick, as a rule. But even an experienced parrot-keeper can occasionally make a mistake in care, producing conditions in which sicknesses occur or are fostered. Moreover, it does happen that for some reason parrots suffer a reduction in their natural resistance, without the keeper's being able to see why or to do anything about it, and this may also result in illness.

Common Signs of Sickness

There are some clearly recognizable signs that indicate a possible illness in a parrot. However, they seldom signal the exact kind of illness, since many ailments do not present an unequivocal picture. In any case, if you notice any symptom in your parrot, you should immediately seek out a veterinarian who specializes in cage-bird illnesses.

A sick parrot has a continually ruffled plumage, rests frequently with head turned back, and exhibits no appetite. In many cases additional symptoms appear, such as frequent sneezing, damp and sticky nostrils, changed feces, or cloudy eyes. As a rule these symptoms indicate a general infection.

First-Aid Measures

Beginning parrot-keepers should never try to treat their Amazons themselves. For them it's always true that the best first aid is a visit to the avian veterinarian at once.

Only a very experienced parrot-keeper can possibly determine whether his Amazon is only slightly sick or whether the symptoms indicate a life-threatening illness. In simple cases he can try to help the Amazon with infrared therapy.

Note: The veterinarian orders infrared or a similar heat therapy for many illnesses (80-85° F or 27-30° C). Therefore every Amazon-keeper should

know how to set it up.

Infrared or similar heat therapy: If several parrots are kept in the same flight cage, the sick bird must be separated from the others in the cage.

For infrared therapy, the parrot is placed in an ordinary parrot cage, which should stand in a separate, bright, quiet, heated room. The infrared or heat lamp should be placed at least 23-1/2 inches (60 cm) from the cage and directed to cover only half the cage so that the parrot can seek out the temperature zone that is most comfortable for it or else can avoid the warmth.

Note: In pet stores there are special "hospital cages" for parrots, which can be warmed and lighted by heat lamps to different temperatures. Depending on your needs, the front consists either of plate glass or wire grating. The floor is a fine-mesh wire grate, which allows the droppings and the food remains to fall through so that they can't be stirred up (which is very important in some diseases).

Feeding: During the period of illness unsweetened, lukewarm camomile tea, Gatorade®,

Infrared illumination is a healing treatment measure for many illnesses. The lamp should only be directed toward half the cage so that the parrot can get out of the warm beams.

honey, or corn syrup added to water (4 tbsp/qt) and soft, vitamin-rich food (for example, sprouted seed, see page 27), and the bird's favorite food should be offered; fruit and green feed should be omitted for the time being.

Caution: If the condition of the parrot does not improve within a few hours, a visit to the avian veterinarian is the only thing left to do!

The Visit to the Avian Veterinarian

If you can't get the address of a veterinarian who has experience with parrots from other parrot-keepers or the pet store dealer, find out by telephone whether the veterinarian of your choice has adequate experience.

Transporting the bird to the veterinarian must be accomplished as quickly as possible. A transport box (see page 18) is most suitable; you should pad it with soft material (crucial to avoid bone-breaking and protect the sick bird).

Important data for the doctor are information about the care and feeding of the Amazon, the time of the appearance of the symptoms, and the course of the illness so far. It will be helpful if you've learned a little about bird illnesses ahead of time (see column to the right and the literature on page 58).

It's best if you take a fecal sample with you, which the veterinarian will usually examine right away. After diagnosis and treatment (often treatment by injection) the veterinarian will as a rule prescribe medication and advise care procedures for the ailing bird. If he or she does not suggest further care, ask whether infrared or heat therapy and soft food (see page 30) would be helpful for the sick Amazon.

The veterinarian will decide the length of the treatment. Follow the doctor's advice exactly, even if the Amazon obviously feels better and begins to jump around in its cage. Relapses are not uncommon when treatment is concluded too soon, and further treatment can then be very difficult.

Common Illnesses

The illnessses described below are frequently caused by mistakes or neglect in care and maintenance or are at least promoted by them:

Infestation with Ectoparasites
(External Parasites)

Parrots can be attacked by mites (*Acarus*), feather mites, or lice. The parasites live on the body surface and in the plumage of the infested bird. In well-kept parrots the infestation is seldom of any great extent.

Symptoms: The infested bird is restless, preens itself often and extensively, and scratches itself frequently with its toes and claws because it is constantly irritated by itching. Bald spots appear on the head, belly, and under the wings by degrees.

Possible causes: Frequent neglect of cleaning procedures; other causes are possible (ask the veterinarian).

Treatment: Dust the bird sparingly with an appropriate insecticide containing pyrethrin or cabaryl (ask advice of the pet dealer or veterinarian) and treat the whole cage.

Caution: To avoid grave poisoning, pay strict attention to the following points:
• Only use an insecticide on which the manufacturer has specifically stated that it is suitable for use on caged birds.
• When dusting the bird, protect the eyes, nose, and beak with your hand.
• Never treat a bird with spray.
• When you are treating the cage, always take the bird out of it.

Prevention: Regular, thorough cleansing of the cage during which all the wooden parts are scrubbed with hot water containing Lysol® (4 oz.

per gallon water) or one-stroke Environ (1/2 oz. per gallon water).

Infestation with Endoparasites
(Internal Parasites)

Parrots are primarily attacked by tapeworms (Cestoda), mawworms (Ascaridia), and hair- or threadworms (Capillaria).

Symptoms: There are no typical manifestations of illness; the ailing bird often sits with ruffled feathers, slowly loses weight, and excretes slimy, thin, and usually foul-smelling stools. Sudden death can occur as the result of an intestinal blockage caused by hundreds of worms (usually mawworms).

Possible causes: Unhygienic maintenance promotes the illness.

Immediate measures: Fecal examination at the first signs of the illness (early treatment can lessen the extent and consequences of worm infestations).

Treatment: By the avian veterinarian. Only he or she can prescribe the proper medication (Dimetridazole, Metronidazole, Levamisole, Yomesan or Piperazine); the directions for use should be followed exactly. An overdose can be dangerous for the parrot.

Prevention: Regularly clean bird cages thoroughly (see above). Have the droppings of parrots who live in a flight cage examined for worms a number of times during the year.

Intestinal Inflammation

One of the most frequent health problems with parrots.

Symptoms: General manifestations of illness (see page 30), diarrhea, increased water intake (as a consequence of the need to replace lost fluids), decreased appetite, so that this illness can signify a serious, sometimes life-threatening risk for the parrot.

Note: Psychological factors can induce a diarrhea-like stool, which is not to be considered a consequence of an intestinal inflammation. Thus,

for example, the sight of a predator hanging in the air or of a cat lurking on the aviary roof, anxiety at being caught by the keeper or at being attacked by a rival parrot can lead to a sudden, watery diarrhea.

Possible causes: Spoiled feed, changed diet, ingestion of poisonous materials (for example, lead, lead weights in curtains, enamel, cleaning materials), colds, attack of parasites, infections.

Immediate measures: Offer camomile tea and soft food, infrared therapy (see page 30). If the bird seems very feeble or if the first aid measures don't lead to improvement within a few hours, take a fecal sample and go to the veterinarian as soon as possible.

Treatment: A treatment by medication must be ordered by the veterinarian. Follow his or her advice exactly!

Prevention: Avoid causes and institute treatment early.

Coccidiosis

Coccidia are one-celled parasites that live in the mucous membranes of the intestinal tract of the parrot.

Symptoms: Coccidia can cause severe inflammation of the mucous membrane, resulting in intestinal bleeding, with accompanying manifestations of diarrhea and weight loss.

Possible causes: Unclean housing conditions and bad health promote the illness.

Treatment: Only the veterinarian can prescribe appropriate medication (Sulfa drugs).

Prevention: Regular, thorough cleaning and disinfecting (according to directions, see above) of the cage area, fecal examination—important because if treatment is begun early, the bird can be free of the coccidia after a short time.

Respiratory Ailments

Disturbances of the respiratory tract can arise from very different causes. A diagnosis is difficult at best and often is impossible in a living bird.

Symptoms: General manifestations of illness

(see page 30), repeated sneezing, damp or stuffed-up nostrils, discharge from the nose, labored breathing (the bird sits with legs spread, breathes with open beak, and the tail moves up and down with every breath), noisy breathing; usually conjunctivitis of the eyelid also occurs.

Possible causes: Attack on the respiratory tract by bacteria, viruses, or fungi; cold from a draft or wrong or suddenly changed maintenance temperature; other causes are also possible.

Immediate measures: Infrared therapy (see page 30). If there is no improvement after 12 hours, the parrot needs veterinary help. With evident breathing difficulty and noisy breathing, go to the avian veterinarian at once!

Treatment: Only by the veterinarian. Early treatment can increase the prospect of healing. Successful treatment is not possible in every case.

Feather Eating, Feather Picking

An uncommon manifestation, which probably belongs to the psychological illnesses. Most often affected are singly kept parrots.

Symptoms: Extension of occasional plucking out and biting of single top feathers, especially in the shoulder or breast area, to the complete balding of the body (with the exception of the unreachable head feathers). There have even been recorded cases of self-mutilation, in which the skin or the musculature beneath it are gnawed.

Possible causes: Inadequately understood, yet until more is determined it is possible to surmise that the coinciding of some of the following factors produces feather eating or picking, or at least promotes it:
• Not enough chance to exercise, such as being kept in a narrow cage.
• Boredom in "sterile quarters."
• Continued stress in close quarters with other birds in one cage or a group in an aviary.
• Missing or wishing for a companion, especially with singly kept parrots.
• Missing a sexual partner at the onset of maturity,

Feather picking. A singly kept parrot is most likely to become a "feather picker." The best remedy is to provide a companion.

especially among aviary and breeding birds.
• Skin diseases that cause itching.
• Inadequate diet, wrong environmental temperature, inadequate humidity
• Lacking opportunities for bathing or lacking regular showers.

Treatment: Correct the mistakes in maintenance and care! In some cases it is wise to move the affected parrot from a cage to a larger flight cage in which there is enough to keep it busy in the form of gnawing branches, chains, wooden playthings, rope ends, or climbing apparatus; if necessary get the bird a companion. Spend more time with your single parrot and make it "quality time"! In our experience, the materials recommended by stores to prevent feather picking as a rule have no effect.

Prevention: Optimum maintenance conditions. For the singly kept parrot, enough attention; better still, furnishing it with a companion.

Parrot Fever (Psittacosis)

Parrot fever or psittacosis is by no means one of the common diseases of parrots. We therefore discuss it only briefly, because the name itself is known to lay people and it can produce serious and to some degree life-threatening manifestations in parrots and humans. Psittacosis is an infectious disease, which in fact does not only affect parrots. The causative agent of this disease has been detected in over one hundred other bird species (in this case one speaks of ornithosis).

Symptoms: No characteristic symptoms. Sleepiness, weight loss, diarrhea, conjunctivitis of the eyelid, and decreased food intake can be accompanying signs of the illness.

Treatment: According to public-health laws the disease must be reported and must be treated. Affected parrots are isolated according to the instructions of the public health officer and treated with an appropriate antibiotic.

Note: A psittacosis infection can become a life-threatening illness in human beings. Besides milder symptoms, something like those of a cold or flu, serious illnesses with high fever and infection of the respiratory tract have also been reported. The disease is curable if it is recognized in time and properly treated.

Precautions: Scarcely possible; it is important that a parrot be free of the pathogen when acquired (you will find further information about psittacosis in the specialists' literature and the newspapers, see page 58). Be careful about buying parrots kept in large lots and under unhygienic conditions.

Breeding Amazons

The Washington Endangered Species Convention

Amazon parrots belong to the bird species that are threatened with extinction. All species are subject to the protection regulations of the Washington Endangered Species Agreement (called WC — Washington Convention — for short), an agreement to which more than 80 countries all over the world have become parties — among them the United States, England, the Netherlands, Australia, and Germany. The WC regulates the traffic in threatened animals and plant species in order to counteract their decline in nature. The threatened animal and plant species are listed in three appendices, according to the degree of endangerment; for each appendix there are special protection regulations. Eleven of the 27 Amazon species are specified in Appendix I of the WC, which means that they are particularly endangered — traffic in them is forbidden. The other Amazon species are covered by the provisions of Appendix II. For trading in these species a legal export license from the native country and an import license are required.

Causes of the disappearance of the Amazons in their natural environment lie primarily in the destruction of their habitat. To gain lumber and arable land the forest districts of the habitat are being recklessly cleared. The brooding and food trees of the Amazon parrots are sacrificed to the power saw or uprooted by gigantic bulldozers. It must also be noted that the trade in the most popular of all of the parrots plays a causative role. Since there are only a very few parrots bred in captivity, wild parrots are still caught by the thousands to supply the Amazon fanciers all over the world. See page 55.

Breeding to Preserve the Species?

We are doubtless scarcely able to undertake anything effective against the destruction of the habitat of the Amazons, but the degree to which the Amazons become captive-bred lessens the number of the imported wild catch by that much. Fortunately the idea of species preservation has recently been attracting more and more attention from parrot fanciers as well as from pet dealers. It is thus agreed that breeding efforts must be intensified for preservation of the Amazon parrot species. Nevertheless, breeding for species preservation — particularly in the case of the Amazon parrot — is no simple matter; the following observations are in order:

• Amazon breeding is still in its infancy. Probabilities of success should not be equated with species protection programs. Reports of successful, consistent breeding attempts that might offer the possibilities of increase in the number of available birds are still very few. Nevertheless, attempts at breeding are being pursued methodically and will eventually certainly lead to success.

• Only when we succeed in breeding Amazons in noticeable numbers will we have taken the first step on the road to species protection.

• Perhaps at some point healthy captive-bred birds should be reestablished in their former distribution ranges to increase the diminished natural supply. In some cases settlement in a substitute biotope will be necessary because of widespread habitat destruction. This challenge is fraught with many difficulties, which need not be discussed here. We hope that the foregoing information will be a spur to as many parrot fanciers as possible to attempt breeding.

• The following instructions for methodical breeding preparations should help you, sooner or later, to be successful in your efforts to reproduce Amazons in captivity.

Legal Requirements for Amazon Breeding

There are no regulations for breeding Amazon parrots in the United States, Canada, or the United

Kingdom. In Germany, Austria, Switzerland, and several other European countries, however, each parrot brood must be reported to the proper authorities. The breeder must file an application "for breeding and trade with parakeets and parrots." Before the application is validated, a federally-appointed veterinarian will examine the applicant on his or her knowledge of breeding, and he will check the purpose in breeding that you have entered on the aforementioned application. Breeders who receive permission are obligated to provide the young birds with official leg bands and must maintain a breeding record book. In this book the details of origin, transfer, illnesses, treatment measures, and death of any of the parrots in question must be entered. After permission has been granted, an inspection of the parrots by a federally-appointed veterinarian will be undertaken at regular intervals.

We feel that this method should be adopted by all countries which embrace the Washington Convention.

Note: When buying breeding animals, also pay attention to the formalities for parrot buying listed on page 12.

Maintenance Conditions for Breeding

The following rules contain the most important requirements, which are determining factors for the success of breeding Amazons:

• You must succeed in putting together two mature, opposite-sexed Amazons of the same variety who are in harmony with each other.

• If possible house the two Amazons together in a separate outdoor aviary with a heated protected area (see page 16) and hang a suitable nest box in the inside room (see page 36). Be careful that the parrots don't keep destroying it.

• Pay attention to the relationship between maintenance temperature, molting, and reproductive cycles (see page 39).

• The feed must be measured and enriched during the breeding period.

The Breeding Pair

It doesn't work to set a male and female (the sexes should be definitely confirmed) in a single cage and then to hope for offspring. The mutual "sympathy" of both parrots is vital for breeding success. If two Amazons do not get along together, they should be separated again after several weeks of trial. It is advantageous for the development of a pair if at any given time several Amazons of one species (if possible from the same subspecies) are available. A pair that develops this way will start out and live in a harmonious, lifelong partnership and will usually raise its young without any untoward incident.

Note: Even parrots of the same sex can form a harmonious "pair"; therefore the sexes of the breeding pair should be definitely confirmed (see page 12).

Housing and Nest Boxes

After partners are chosen it's advisable to give each pair a separate cage in which it will not be disturbed by its fellow birds. Otherwise at the beginning of the mating period serious clashes can occur between rival Amazons, which — for want of the possibility of escape in a cage — can sometimes end in death.

The nest box is best placed in the inner room for protection from cold, wind, and dampness — if possible attached high under the roof. For all the Amazons described in this book nest boxes with the

Parrots are skillful climbers.
A yellow-naped Amazon (*Amazona ochrocephala auropalliata*) and a bright scarlet Ara (*Ara macao*) in their natural habitat.

following dimensions will be suitable: height, 31 to 39 inches (80-100 cm); inside diameter, 12 to 14 inches (30-35 cm), hole diameter, 4 to 5 inches (10-12 cm). (The white-fronted Amazons (*Amazona albifrons*) will also put up with smaller boxes.) You can find practical nest boxes in the pet shop. They have an opening in the lower portion through which you can see into the box to check on the young birds or to take out dead eggs. A layer of soft humus will allow for the proper positioning of the eggs under the weight of the brooding Amazon female.

Note: After the brooding period remove the nest box, clean it, disinfect it, repair if necessary, and let it dry until the beginning of the next breeding period.

Maintenance Temperature During Molting and Reproductive Cycles

In parrots there exists an important relationship between the maintenance temperature, the breeding cycle, and the molting season: As a rule, parrots do not breed during the molting period. The parrots must get used to a rhythm of life in which breeding can be completed at a time that is suited to our widely fluctuating climate (i.e., in summer) and molting begun right afterward. This rhythm can be achieved by manipulating the maintenance conditions.

The following seasonal rhythm is necessary: In April/May, when it slowly becomes warmer in various parts of the United States, with the exception of Florida or California, where *year-round* breeding is possible, the courtship period must begin. Egg-laying and brooding should take place in early summer; raising the young may last until the end of September. After that, molting must take

Acrobatic feats while getting food — yellow-necked Amazon in her natural habitat.

place for four to eight weeks so that before the beginning of winter the parrots can replace the feathers that have become tattered during brooding with new ones and, again completely and warmly protected, survive the winter well. This is how this seasonal rhythm is achieved: In winter and spring, from the beginning of November to the beginning of April, the lodgings of the parrots are only warmed to about 43° to 46°F (6-8°C). The beginning of the war season brings the parrots into the breeding mood, and they begin the business of mating. Molting then occurs — as desired—in the fall. Though two years is the average length of time it takes to adapt to these conditions of seasonal rhythm favorable for breeding, once established, the rhythm will thenceforth be maintained.

Caution: Caged birds that are used to warmth and freshly imported Amazons must slowly become used to the lower maintenance temperatures described above over the course of several months!

Feeding of Breeding Birds

In the winter months parrots that are to be bred receive the usual allotment of parrot food (see Proper Feeding, page 29). Before the onset of the breeding period the food will be enriched by the addition of stimulating nutrient elements, such as sprouted seed or legumes that have been soaked and then cooked, to bring the birds to breeding pitch. At the same time it is advisable to get the birds used to the addition of a vitamin- and protein-rich nourishing food that contains all the important nutrients for the young (see Breeding Food, page 28).

Courtship and Mating

With the onset of the warmer weather, sometimes as early as April but usually not until early in May, Amazons begin courting. With newly paired Amazons it can go along quite conspicuously and at loud volume (for detailed description of courtship behavior, see page 45). Abundant social grooming, loud cries, and irresolute attempts by the male to feed the female (partner feeding, sometimes also called courtship feeding) accompany the courtship, which usually will last several days but sometimes also lasts a few weeks. With older pairs, who have already gone through breeding a number of times, some elements of the breeding pattern disappear. In some instances spontaneous mating may even occur without any preliminary wooing (see Copulation, page 45).

The courtship period comes to an end with the first copulation. The matings, which sometimes last for many seconds, become increasingly frequent.

Appropriate breeding holes: Left: Hollowed-out tree trunk (available in pet store); its examination door is cut out of the side and closed with a metal pin. Right: Homemade nest box. Roof and examination door can be raised.

Egg Laying and Brooding

If the female remains squatting in the nest hole for hours at a time and produces noticeably large quantities of droppings, these are signs that egg laying is imminent. In captivity, mostly at the end of May or the beginning of June, Amazon parrots lay two to four pure white eggs on the humus covering of the nest-box floor.

With the laying of the second egg the female begins her brooding, which — depending on weather and brooding activity — may take 26 to 28 days. Mostly the female broods alone, but sometimes the male squats beside the female in the nest box or else visits the female there to supply her with food.

Hatching and Rearing the Young

The young hatch at the same intervals as the eggs were laid. The female may provide help by picking at the egg shell. Newly hatched Amazons are — like all altricial birds — naked, barely fluffy, blind, and extremely helpless. They need between 70 to 100 days before they resemble the parents in size and weight, have developed a complete plumage, and are in a position to find their own food. In this period both parents have much to do with the feeding.

Feeding the Young: The male takes food from the feeding dishes and swallows it into his crop, where the first digestive process begins. He then feeds the predigested gruel-like food to his mate, who eventually regurgitates it — again predigested in the crop — and gives it to the young. In the first weeks of life young parrots have a broadened, shovel-shaped lower mandible, into which the female puts the food, initially a thin fluid. Later, when the babies are older, the male also takes a direct part in the feeding.

During the feeding process the feeding parent crosses its own beak with that of the young bird, regurgitates the food from its crop with pumping neck movements, and transfers it to the young bird with shaking, back-and-forth movements.

Hand-Feeding

It often happens that Amazon parrots — especially inexperienced first-time breeders — destroy eggs and kill newly hatched birds or leave the eggs because of frequent disturbances. In this last case you have the chance — if you recognize the situation in time — to bring the eggs along to further de-

Three young at the age of 7, 9, and 10 days — their eyes are still closed; they open between the 15th and the 26th day.

Egg tooth

Young bird 15 days old — the first quills are becoming visible on the wings.

Amazon at the age of 26 days — the plumage on the wings, head, and tail is now clearly to be seen.

velopment in an incubator and to raise the hatched babies—or the abandoned young birds — by hand. This possibility should only be viewed as a solution of necessity, because hand-raised young birds develop an attachment for humans in earliest infancy and are then very difficult to use later for breeding purposes. A committed parrot fancier will not resort to hand-raising merely to get tame, dependent young birds.

If the parents no longer visit the nest box and the danger arises that the young birds will die, the keeper must of course intervene and help.

Maintenance: Parrot chicks should be kept in a tank that is warmed to about 96.8°F (36°C); infrared lamps and the hospital cage described on page 30 serve very well.

Feeding and Food: In the beginning the young parrots are provided with food about every two hours between 6AM and 12PM. With newly hatched parrots the feeding is not begun until the second day. Powdered baby food is good for feeding material. It is mixed with water and at two- to three-day intervals vitamin and mineral supplements are mixed in. At feeding time the mixture must be at a temperature of 104°to 106°F (40°- 41°C). It must be mixed fresh daily.

Hand-feeding. A young bird that has been abandoned by its parents can be raised by hand. The young bird is given the feed gruel with a teaspoon.

Breeding Amazons

As the birds get older, the intervals between feedings can be lengthened to about every three or four hours, the gruel can be thickened a bit with finely minced egg yolk, fruit, and vegetables, and its temperature lowered to lukewarm.

It is difficult to manage the crossover from gruel to solid seed feed. You should therefore accustom the young Amazon step by step to eating out of the feeding dish. In the beginning it should find its usual gruel there, then later soft fruit and greenery, and finally seeds as well. To teach the young bird how to remove the hulls from the seed, it's good if it can watch how another bird in a neighboring cage does so. Monitor the temperature of the environment; drafts and sudden temperature changes are injurious to young birds. Only when their plumage is complete can they be maintained at room temperature without additional sources of heat.

Understanding Amazons

How Amazons Live Together in Nature

By nature, Amazon parrots are very social birds. In their natural habitat they live together in groups and order their behavior in reference to their fellow Amazons.

The group size depends upon the food supply and the purpose of the grouping (for example, food-seeking, or sleeping companions). With the exception of the breeding season and in times of abundant plant and fruit growth, frequently gigantic swarms, which can include several hundred birds, are found together. Many times they go on searches for food together, often flying distances of many miles daily, to systematically harvest their favorite fruit or fruit parts from tree to tree. Some Amazons have developed into regular migrants, who change their location several times a year depending on the fruit harvest. Others are more or less permanently located but daily undertake extended flights to their feeding grounds.

Before dusk falls, the Amazons fly back to their roosting place for the night. Depending on the size of the group they use one sleeping tree in common or several trees close together, into which they crowd and loudly defend their perches against one another.

Permanent pair bonding is entered into only with the onset of sexual maturity. Amazon pairs are usually easy to pick out during flight and at roosting because they stick closely together and there is much body contact. Young birds and subadult (not yet sexually mature) Amazons frequently group together in flocks of young birds, in which the pairs later meet. This pairing is not yet sexually motivated; it can be regarded as a kind of engagement period.

At the beginning of the breeding period Amazons change their behavior in the group. They become increasingly aggressive toward their comrades, defend their sleeping places, and separate themselves more and more from the group. In a somewhat removed breeding area the pair occupies its own nesting hole and probably also territory, which they energetically defend against any intruder. For breeding holes Amazon parrots use abandoned woodpecker holes or rotted-out tree holes, which they widen with their strong beaks. The wood chips that fall on the hole floor as well as the decayed wood that is already there will not be removed from the nesting space but will serve as the proper medium for the eggs and to keep the required high humidity in the hole constant.

Egg laying follows courtship. Depending on the species, the female lays 2 to 5 eggs, which are brooded for 26 to 28 days.

Raising the young lasts for 10 to 14 weeks. When the young are independent, the small family band separates and the parents rejoin the other parrots in a group. The young birds remain in the vicinity of the parents for a while longer but become increasingly independent and sooner or later join together with parrots of the same age.

Important Behavior Patterns of Amazons

So far, unfortunately, we know very little about the behavior of the Amazon; scientific behavior studies still do not exist. To help the Amazon-keeper learn to understand his Amazon better and to stimulate him to make his own observations, we report on the most frequently noted behavior patterns of Amazons.

How Amazons Propel Themselves

Amazons love to climb; one gets the impression with those in cages and aviaries that climbing is the preferred way of movement for Amazon parrots. Still, you should not undervalue their flying capabilities and their need to fly, especially if you remember that many Amazons undertake long flights in the search for food. In roomy flight cages it is possible to observe that they make active, enthusiastic use of their wings. Many species, like the white-fronted (*A. albifrons*), green-cheeked (A. *viridigenalis*), lilac-crowned (*A. finschi*), and orange-winged (*A. amazonica*) Amazons are very skillful fliers, while the blue-fronted (*A. aestiva*) and some varieties of the yellow-crowned Amazon fly cumbersomely ("helicopter-like"). In any case, Amazons have a great urge to fly. The parrot-keeper must provide enough opportunities for exercise. Amazons go along the ground only reluctantly, and even on flat surfaces they move clumsily with toes turned in pigeon-toed.

Feeding

Seeds are hulled in the beak with the help of the tongue, fruit and green feed minced with the beak. All the food is first stored in the crop and predigested before it is conveyed to the other digestive system for utilization.

Like almost all large parrots, the Amazon also uses its foot like a hand to grasp large pieces of food and to hold them to its beak for breaking into smaller pieces.

Amazons waste their food profligately, which every parrot-keeper must learn to get used to; they nibble fruit and then leave it unnoticed; some root through the food bowl for favorite seeds and knock the less liked kernels out of the dish with one "beak stroke."

Body Care

Amazons preen their feathers many times a day; the individual feathers are drawn through the beak and thus cleaned. The Amazon removes dirt and feather fragments from its beak by rubbing it on a hard surface, such as the perch. The toes are cleaned with the beak. To help with body care, the Amazon in captivity also needs a shower bath or a bathing tub filled with water. (See The Shower Bath, page 23 for information on bathing a parrot in your home.) Unfortunately, there seems to be no way to break Amazon parrots of this unsightly feeding pattern.

Preening. Amazons preen their feathers several times daily; in the process the individual feathers are pulled through the beak and thus cleaned.

Social Behavior

In their communal life with other birds Amazons display very pronounced behavior patterns, which are often impressive for the observer.

Social Preening

The mutual scratching and preening of the feathers does two things for parrots: In the first place, head and undertail-coverts, which the parrot cannot reach with its own beak, are cleaned by the partner. And second, the social grooming has an important function in pairing and bonding. In conflict situations it is frequently observed that Amazons sit close together and mutually preen their feathers, obviously to reconfirm the partnership.

In critical situations, for example if a dog or an unknown human approaches, in which one would really expect a reaction like flight or attack, they first scratch each other before they respond according to the situation.

Understanding Amazons

Courtship Behavior

Besides social preening there is a whole list of other behavior patterns that are part of the courtship behavior of Amazons:

Display Behavior: The Amazon male secures his breeding territory — even in an aviary—well in advance and protects it with striking behavior. On an exposed place in his territory, he struts, often screaming loudly, in an upright stance with wings spread and tail feathers spreading open and closed. This has a terrifying effect on rival Amazons and also on birds of related parrot species. The impression is strengthened by optical signals provided by opening his wings and spreading his tail, displaying the extraordinary feather colors, which are in strong contrast to the usual mostly green color of the body plumage.

With time the aggressive mood of the male increases, and the display and threatening behavior is followed by a period of readiness to attack. Now fellow aviary inhabitants and even the keeper may become the victims of dangerous attacks, which not uncommonly conclude fatally for the fellow inhabitants of the aviary and for the humans often bloodily. During brooding the male also secures the food supply against competition and protects the

Yawning Amazons. Parrots yawn when they are tired, to take in oxygen, or to stretch their beaks. An Amazon pair often exhibits the same behavior gesture at the same time like this pair yawning.

nest hole, female, and later the young birds from enemies.

The display behavior increases even more; besides the opening wings and spreading tail, the neck and upper back feathers will also be spread from time to time. The male thus struts here and there, turning this way and that in order to be seen from all sides. In addition, from time to time he demonstrates his beak strength by biting off wood splinters from his climbing branches with powerful beak movements and throwing them to the ground.

If the chosen female appears, it looks as if the male tries to intensify his efforts. Striking a still larger and more upright pose, he seeks the favor of the female, still more readily and aggressively attacks his aviary neighbors, and will be "egged on" by the loud, almost encouraging-sounding screams of the female. At this moment the display behavior is at its most striking. The female takes the wooing attempts of the male very coolly at first and evades his attempts at copulation, at first growling strongly or resisting; with time, however, she suffers his approaches. The social preening creates diminished aggression and pair-bonding. It is an important component of courtship.

Partner Feeding: Shortly before copulation yet another behavior appears, which like social preening has a two-fold function: partner feeding, which now is observable particularly often. On the one hand it serves as an aggression-diminishing element to strengthen the pair bond; on the other the male is trying out his inborn feeding mechanism. With pumping movements he regurgitates a stream of predigested food from his crop and tries to give this to the female. It sometimes takes a while before this process functions smoothly. Only if the food transfer works successfully, however, can it be guaranteed that later, during the brooding and raising of young, the female and the young birds will be able to receive nourishment from the male in sufficient amounts.

Copulation: The courtship period lasts only a few days, sometimes a few weeks; the female finally no longer avoids the male's attempts to get near her and invites mating with submissive posture and trembling, spread wings. With copulation the courtship period comes to an end and a few days later, after successful egg laying, the female begins brooding. After 26 to 28 days the young appear.

How Amazons Threaten Opponents

Amazons live relatively peacefully with each other; great battles, which end with wounds or even death of the opponent, seldom occur. But since the space in an aviary is scarcely large enough for a courting and displaying Amazon male, fights there are not entirely out of the question. Smaller quarrels about food or rest and sleeping places are observable the whole year through. If one Amazon advances too close to another, he will threaten with a raised foot, to keep the "intruder" at a distance. If the threatened Amazon does not observe this "request," it can result in a regular footfight. Neither of the contestants will be wounded by this; the defeated one as a rule will yield his place after the quarrel. What looks threatening to the observer is the beak fight, in which the attacker directs his beak against the head, shoulders, and beak of the opponent, which the attacked one mostly parries. But both birds remain uninjured, because the natural social biting inhibition hinders serious biting, even though there are many chances to do so.

Note: If it comes to frequent conflicts between two Amazons over a long period of time, the keeper should separate the birds and try to place each of them with a different partner.

Strikingly colored Amazon species.
Above left: Vinaceous Amazon (*Amazona vinacea*)—not available in trade, it is listed in Appendix I, the "Red List" of the WC (Washington Convention); above right: Yellow-cheeked Amazon (*Amazona autumnalis autumnalis*); below left: White-fronted Amazon (*Amazona albifrons*); below right: Yellow-headed Amazon (*Amazona ochrocephala belizensis*).

Popular Amazon Species

Some Facts About Amazons

Amazon parrots, with around 330 genera, form a single order among the some 8,600 genera constituting the vertebrate class of birds. Parrots are differentiated very distinctly from other bird groups by their body build, the curved beak, the toe position (two toes aim forward, two rearward), and the grasping foot. Their closest relatives are the owls, the doves, and the cuckoos.

Parrots live in all parts of the earth with the exception of Europe. They dwell predominantly in the tropical and subtropical climate zones; only a few species live in barren regions, which are sought temporarily at times of frost or snowfall.

The Genus Amazon: The Amazon parrots were described scientifically for the first time by Lesson. They have the Latin genus name *Amazona*. To this group belong 27 medium-large to large parrot species, which are mostly green in color and have a short, rounded tail. They are also known as blunt-tailed parrots.

Range: Amazon parrots occur only in South and Central America, including the West Indies. In the north the distribution range of several species (lilac-crowned [*A. finschi*], white-fronted [*A. albifrons*], green-cheeked [*A. viridigenalis*], yellow-cheeked or red-crowned Amazons) extends up to Mexico and the borders of the United States. In the south the yellow-winged varieties of the blue-fronted Amazon reaches to northeastern Argentina and the northwestern tip of Uruguay. The majority of species are concentrated in the tropical climate zone between the northern and southern tropics. Their distribution range embraces a linear area from north to south of more than 3,000 miles (5,000 kilometers).

Tropical forest climates with constant high temperatures and humidity as well as tropical savannah climates with short dry periods characterize the regions in which Amazon parrots are at home.

Frequently Kept Amazon Species

In the past almost all of the 27 Amazon species were imported to Europe and the U.S.A. at one time or another in more or less large numbers. Because of the species protection laws (see page 35), today only a few species are regularly imported, for example, orange-winged, blue-fronted, and Mealy Amazons. Other species (yellow-crowned [*A. ochro-cephala*], white-fronted [*A.albifrons*], green-cheeked [*A.viridigenalis*], lilac-crowned [*A. finschi*], and red-lored [*A. autumnalis*] Amazons) appear significantly less often in trade. All named species may — in accordance with the provisions of the animal protection laws — be imported. They are described in detail below.

Orange-winged Amazon

Amazona amazonica (3 subspecies)

[Photograph: page 48]

Description: Total length 12-1/2 inches (32 cm); male and female: basic plumage color green; brow and crown irregularly blue-yellow; cheeks

Orange-winged Amazon (*Amazona amazonica*).

yellow; edges of wings yellow-green; wing speculum red; tail feathers green, the interiors of the outermost feathers partly red; beak horn-colored, darker at the tip; feet gray; unfeathered eye ring gray; iris yellow-orange. The young are similar to their parents, but the iris is dark brown.

Range: All of northern South America with the exception of the Andes areas in the west and the coastal districts of eastern Brazil; in the south, in parts of Bolivia and in the northern tip of Paraguay.

Habitat: Damp woods and mangrove swamp areas.

Character: One of the most often imported of all Amazon species. Easy to tame, teachable, but less "speech-gifted" species, which is good for keeping in a cage and also in an outdoor aviary and is little prone to illness; in a roomy aviary several can be kept together.

Breeding: Only successful a few times; a breeder in Tampa, Florida raised three chicks by hand in 1970; first German breeding in 1978 in Weil am Rhein. Clutch of 2 to 3 eggs, brooding time 28 days, nestling period 8 to 10 weeks; young birds are largely green, with only the beginnings of a few blue and yellow feathers in the head region.

Blue-fronted Amazon

Amazona aestiva (2 subspecies)
[Photographs: front cover, inside front and inside back cover, back cover.]

Description: Total length 14 inches (37 cm); male and female: basic plumage color green; forehead and bridle bright blue; crown, eye region, in some birds also the throat, breast front, and upper leg yellow; unfeathered eye ring gray-blue; front edge of wings red, usually shot through with yellow; wing speculum and tail feathers red at the base; beak black; feet blue-gray; iris red to orange. In the subspecies *Amazona aestiva xanthopteryx*, the edges of the wings are yellow, mixed with red, although in some birds the red is entirely replaced by yellow.

Range: The nominate form is in northeastern Brazil to Paraguay and the northern parts of Argentina; the variety *Amazona aestiva xanthopteryx* ranges from northern Bolivia, parts of Brazil, Paraguay, and northern Argentina to northernmost Buenos Aires.

Habitat: Preponderantly forests in tropical and subtropical climate zones.

Character: A popular species and known for decades. Easily tameable, good talent for imitation but also makes natural sounds that are impossible to ignore; robust and hardy in cage and aviary. Frequently behavioral changes occur with the onset of sexual maturity, particularly in single birds: increase in aggressiveness, courting, attempts to copulate, and false brooding in room cages; neurotic stereotypical movements, sometimes a tendency to feather picking.

Breeding: Frequently successful, but because of large numbers of imports not much attempted.

Several successful attempts were made a number of years ago. In spite of positive outcome, however, there are by no means always breeding birds available in captivity. Sex determination is difficult, but adult females are likely to have red irises, males orange ones. Clutch of 2 to 5 eggs, brooding time 28 days, nestling time 55 to 60 days; young birds similar to adult animals except that all the colors are duller.

Popular Amazon Species

Mealy Amazon
Amazona farinosa (5 subspecies)
[Photograph page 10]

Description: Total length 15 to 15-1/2 inches (38-40 cm). Male and female: basic plumage color green; upper side green, dusted with gray; some

feathers on the crown are yellow; wing edges and speculum red; yellowish-green band at the end of the tail; unfeathered eye ring white; beak a dark horn color with a yellow area at the base of the upper mandible; feet gray; iris red-brown. The variety *Amazona farinosa inornata* lacks the yellow on the crown area; the crown and the neck of the Amazona *farinosa guatemalae* are bluish.

Range: From Mexico in the north to the southern Atlantic coast of Brazil in the south; in the northwestern part of South America.

Habitat: Sparse rain forests and the forest border zone; thick tropical forests are largely shunned.

Character: At the moment this is probably the most commonly seen species in the European trade, with a quiet, apparently "harmonious" nature, comfortable movements, but piercing screams. It is extremely popular in the United States also. Quickly becomes tame and gets along well with other Amazons. It is hardy and so is well suited for outdoor aviary keeping.

Breeding: Until now scarcely successful; first German attempt (*Amazona farinosa guatemalae*) in 1984 by Dr. W. Burkhard, Benningen, Switzerland; a clutch of 3 eggs was laid; brooding time about 28 days, nestling period about 8 weeks.

Yellow-crowned Amazon
Amazona ochrocephala (9 subspecies)
[Photographs pages 10, 11, 37, and 47]

Description: Total length 13-1/2 inches (35 cm); male and female: basic plumage color green; wing edge and wing speculum bright red; underside of tail yellowish green with a red spot at the base of each tail feather; beak dark gray, base and portion of upper mandible pink; feet gray; unfeathered eye ring white; iris orange.

Range: South America from the Guyanas and Venezuela in the east to the Colombian Andes in the west; island of Trinidad.

Amazona ochrocephala panamensis resembles the nominate form but the forehead is yellow, the beak is horn-colored with a darker point on the upper mandible, the feet are flesh-colored; it is smaller (13 inches [33 cm]).

Range: Panama and the tropical lowlands in northern Colombia.

Amazona ochrocephala auropalliata resembles the nominate form, except the neck portion is yellow, the beak is horn-colored gray, the eye ring is gray, the feet flesh-colored; it is larger (15 inches [39 cm]).

Range: Central America, from southwestern Mexico in the north to Costa Rica in the south.

Amazona ochrocephala oratrix resembles the nominate form except the head and neck are yellow, the beak is horn-colored, the feet are brighter; it is larger (16 inches [41 cm]).

Range: Mexico.

Amazona ochrocephala belizensis resembles the oratrix subspecies except for a less extensive area of yellow on the head.

Range: Honduras.

Popular Amazon Species

The other subspecies occur singly or are unknown in the trade.

Some very freqently kept varieties have acquired their own English names:

• *Amazona ochrocephala ochrocephala*: Surinam Amazon

• *Amazona ochrocephala panamensis*: Panama yellow-headed Amazon

• *Amazona ochrocephala auropalliata*: Yellow-naped or Golden-naped Amazon

• *Amazona ochrocephala oratrix*: Double yellow-fronted or Mexican yellow-headed Amazon; and *Amazona ochrocephala belizensis*: Double yellow-headed Amazon of British Honduras.

Character: Rarely imported now, but because of large quantities imported in earlier days seen very frequently all over. Robust, hardy cage and aviary birds; all varieties are easy to tame and possess an extraordinary talent for mimicry but also a very loud natural voice, which manifests itself even more strongly during the mating period.

Breeding: Often successful with a number of varieties. Clutches of 3 to 4 eggs, brooding time 26 to 28 days, nestling period 12 weeks.

White-fronted or White-browed Amazon, or Spectacled Amazon Parrot

Amazona albifrons (3 subspecies)
[Photographs pages 20 and 47]

Description: Total length 10 inches (27 cm); male: basic plumage color green; forehead white; crown green-blue; eye area and bridle red; unfeathered eye ring gray-white; wing edges red; beak yellowish; legs bright gray; iris yellowish; female: resembles the male but without the red wing edge

(alula). Immature males have a green alula and the white color of the forehead and forecrown is tinged with yellow.

Range: From the west coast of Mexico across Guatemala, Honduras, and El Salvador to Costa Rica.

Habitat: Dry bush and deciduous forests; only occasionally tropical rain-forest areas.

Character: Scarcely seen in trade anymore; females always in the minority. Young birds are, as already stated, recognizable by a dark iris and above all by the yellowish color on the forehead instead of white. Kept singly they should quickly become tame and reveal a noteworthy "speaking ability"; kept in an aviary they are mostly shy and fearful; in a roomy aviary they are skillful fliers.

Breeding: Males and females are differentiated in color. First German breeding attempt by H. Muller, of Walsrode, in 1977; since then successful breeding by several parrot fanciers including some in the United States; clutches of 3 to 4, and in exceptional cases 5 eggs; length of brooding 28 days, nestling period about 70 days.

Popular Amazon Species

Green-cheeked or red-crowned Amazon

Amazona viridigenalis
[Photograph page 10]

Description: Total length 13 inches (33 cm); male and female: basic plumage color green; forehead and crown red; half-moon-shaped blue-violet band in the cheek area; primary coverts blue and red; beak yellowish, with white cere; unfeathered eye ring white; legs gray; iris yellow.

Range: Northeastern Mexico exclusively.

Habitat: Forest areas along rivers, grain-cultivating districts in damp lowlands, sparse, dry, pine-covered mountain ridges, tropical forests of the canyons.

Character: No longer imported in Europe; usually animals come into trade from private hands and among them are some captive-bred birds. Less suitable for keeping in a cage, there single birds are very inactive; also in an outdoor aviary less lively than other species; have piercing cries.

Breeding: Adult males and females are clearly differentiated because of the different dimensions of the red head patch which is less extensive in the female. First breeding in 1970 in Africa and England; first German attempt in 1982 by the authors of this book; clutch 2 to 3 eggs, brooding period 28 days, nestling period about 70 days, independent eating at about 120 days.

Lilac-crowned or Finsch Amazon

Amazona finschi (2 subspecies)
[Photograph page 10]

Description: Total length 13 inches (33 cm); male and female: basic plumage color green, neck and upper side with black margins; forehead and bridle red-brown; crown, neck, and half-moon around cheek feathers bluish-white; wings blue-black; beak horn-colored; feet gray; iris orange.

Range: Western Mexico.

Habitat: Plains, forested mountain regions up to heights of about 7,200 feet (2,200 meters), occasionally in grain fields and banana plantations.

Character: Last large import around 1980; no more imported since. In behavior similar to the green-cheeked Amazon [*A. viridigenalis*], but livelier; very nimble flier; less suited for keeping in a cage, although young birds can become tame.

Breeding: Until now isolated attempts at hand breeding have been successful only in English-speaking areas; brooding time probably 28 days; nestling period around 60 to 70 days.

Red-lored Amazon

Amazona autumnalis (4 subspecies)
[Photographs pages 9, 19, and 47]

Description: Total length 13 inches (34 cm); male and female: basic plumage color green; fore-

Popular Amazon Species

head and bridle scarlet red; crown and individual neck feathers bright blue; cheeks yellow; wing speculum red; wing pinion blue-black; beak dark horn-colored; feet gray; unfeathered eye ring white; iris gold-brown to dark brown; the subspecies *Amazona autumnalis salvini* (Salvin's Amazon) lacks the yellow cheek color; in *Amazona autumnalis lilacina* (Ecuador Amazon) the crown is blue-violet, the ear region green; *Amazona autumnalis diadema* (diademed Amazon) resembles Salvin's Amazon but differs from it mainly in the thick, red, hairlike feathers of the nose area.

Range: The nominate form along the east coast of Mexico to the peninsula of Belize, Guatemala, and Honduras; Amazona *autumnalis salvini* in Nicaragua, Costa Rica, Panama, and the west coast of Colombia; *Amazona autumnalis lilacina* only in Ecuador; *Amazona autumnalis diadema* in interior Brazil.

Habitat: Tropical lowland forests and forest border zones.

Character: Red-lored Amazons appear occasionally, Salvin's and Ecuador Amazons very seldom, and diademed Amazons never in the trade; the occasional birds available are mostly from private owners. All known varieties get used to cage and

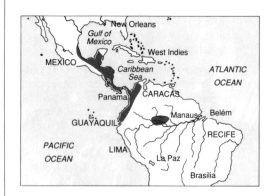

aviary living well; they are easily tamed and have an agreeable manner. Their "speaking ability" is not particularly large; their own cries are piercing and monotonous.

Breeding: Only isolated successes; first successful attempt with the Ecuador Amazon in 1946 in the U.S.A., with the nominate form in 1956 in England; first breeding in Germany in 1983 by S. Maindok, Alzey (nominate form) and by K.H. Uhlenkott, Ahaus (probably Salvin's Amazon); clutches of 3 eggs; brooding time 26 to 28 days, no exact details about nestling periods.

Bringing Birds into the USA

What is a Pet Bird?

A pet bird is defined as any bird, except poultry, intended for the personal pleasure of its individual owner, not for resale. Poultry, even if kept as pets, are imported under separate rules and quarantined at USDA animal import centers. Birds classified as poultry include chickens, turkeys, pheasants, partridge, ducks, geese, swans, doves, peafowl, and similar avian species.

Importing a Pet Bird

Special rules for bringing a pet bird into the United States (from all countries but Canada):
• USDA quarantine
• Quarantine/space reservation
• Fee in advance
• Foreign health certificate
• Final shipping arrangements
• Two-bird limit

To bring pet birds into the country, you must:
Quarantine your bird (or birds) for at least 30 days in a USDA-operated import facility at one of nine ports of entry. The bird, which must be caged when you bring it in, will be transferred to a special isolation cage at the import facility.

Reserve quarantine space for the bird. A bird without a reservation will be accepted only if space is available. If none exists, this bird will either be refused entry or be transported, at your expense, to another port where there is space.

Pay the USDA an advance fee of $40 to be applied to the cost of quarantine services and necessary tests and examinations. Currently, quarantine costs are expected to average $80 for one bird or $100 per isolation cage if more than one bird is put in the cage. These charges may change without notice. You may also have to pay private companies for brokerage and transportation services to move the bird from one port of entry to the USDA import facility.

Obtain a health certificate in the nation of the bird's origin. This is a certificate signed by a national government veterinarian stating that the bird has been examined, shows no evidence of communicable disease, and is being exported in accordance with the laws of that country. The certificate must be signed within 30 days of the time the bird arrives in the United States. If not in English, it must be translated at your cost.

Arrange for shipping the bird to its final destination when it is released from quarantine. A list of brokers for each of the nine ports of entry may be requested from USDA ports veterinarians at the time quarantine space is reserved. (See addresses to follow.) Most brokers offer transportation services from entry ports to final destination.

Bring no more than two psittacine birds (parrots, parakeets, and other hookbills) per family into the United States during any single year. Larger groups of these birds are imported under separate rules for commercial shipment of birds.

Ports of Entry for Personally Owned Pet Birds

Listed below are the nine ports of entry for personally owned pet birds. To reserve quarantine space for your bird, write to the port veterinarian at the city where you'll be arriving and request Form 17-23. Return the completed form, together with a check or money order (contact veterinarian in charge of the import facility for current cost) made payable to USDA, to the same address. The balance of the fee will be due before the bird is released from quarantine.

Port Veterinarian Animal and Plant Health Inspection Service (APHIS) U.S. Department of Agriculture (City, State, Zip Code)
New York, New York 11430
Miami, Florida 33152
Laredo, Texas 78040
El Paso, Texas 79902
Nogales, Arizona 85621
San Ysidro, California (Mailing address, Lawndale, CA 90261)
Honolulu, Hawaii 96850

Bringing Birds into the USA

The Quarantine Period

During quarantine, pet birds will be kept in individually controlled isolation cages to prevent any infection from spreading. Psittacine or hook-billed birds will be identified with a leg band. They will be fed a medicated feed as required by the U.S. Public Health Service to prevent psittacosis, a flu-like disease transmittable to humans. Food and water will be readily available to the birds. Young, immature birds needing daily hand-feeding cannot be accepted because removing them from the isolation cage for feeding would interrupt the 30-day quarantine. During the quarantine, APHIS veterinarians will test the birds to make certain they are free of any communicable disease of poultry. Infected birds will be refused entry; at the owner's option they will be returned to the country of origin (at the owner's expense) or humanely destroyed.

Special Exceptions

No government quarantine (and therefore no advance reservations or fees) and no foreign health certificate are required for:

• *U.S. birds taken out of the country if special arrangements are made in advance.* Before leaving the United States, you must gain a health certificate for the bird from a veterinarian accredited by the USDA and make certain it is identified with a tattoo or numbered leg band. The health certificate, with this identification on it, must be presented at the time of re-entry. While out of the country, you must keep your bird separate from other birds. Remember that only two psittacine or hookbilled birds per family per year may enter the United States. Birds returning to the United States may come through any one of nine ports of entry listed earlier. There are also certain other specified ports of entry for these birds, depending upon the time of arrival and other factors. Contact APHIS officials for information on this prior to leaving the country.

• *Birds from Canada.* Pet birds may enter the United States from Canada on your signed statement that they have been in your possession for at least 90 days, were kept separate from other birds during the period, and are healthy. As with other countries, only two psittacine birds per family per year may enter the United States from Canada. Birds must be inspected by an APHIS veterinarian at designated ports of entry for land, air, and ocean shipments. These ports are subject to change, so for current information, contact APHIS/USDA.

Pet birds from Canada are not quarantined because Canada's animal disease control and eradication programs and import rules are similar to those of the United States.

Other U.S. Agencies Involved

In addition to the U.S. Public Health Service requirement mentioned ealier, U.S. Department of the Interior rules require an inspection by one of its officials to assure that an imported bird is not in the rare or endangered species category, is not an illegally imported migratory bird, and is not an agricultural pest or injurious to humans. For details from these agencies, contact:

Division of Law Enforcement, Fish and Wildlife Service, U.S. Department of the Interior Washington, D.C. 20240

Bureau of Epidemiology, Quarantine Division, Center for Disease Control, U.S. Public Health Service, Atlanta, Georgia 30333

U.S. Customs Service, Department of the Treasury, Washington, D.C. 20229

For additional information on USDA-APHIS regulations, contact,

Import-Export Staff,
Veterinary Services, APHIS
U.S. Department of Agriculture,
Hyattsville, Maryland 20782

Endangered and Extinct Species

Parrot Species in Danger of Extinction

Appendix I of the Washington Convention lists all the parrots that are in immediate danger of extinction or close to it. Trade in these birds is prohibited except for parrots that were raised in captivity. The most recent edition of Appendix I, drawn up at the fifth conference of May 1985, includes the following species.

Amazona versicolor, versicolor or St. Lucia Amazon

Amazona vinacea, vinaceous Amazon

Amazona vittata, Puerto Rican Amazon

Anadorhynchus glaucus, glaucous macaw (may be extinct)

Anadorhynchus leari, Lear's macaw

Ara rubrogenys, red-fronted or red-crowned macaw

Ara glaucogularis, blue-throated macaw

Ara ambigua, great green macaw

Ara macao, scarlet macaw

Arantinga guarouba, golden conure

Cyanopsitta spixii, Spix's macaw

Cyanoramphus auriceps forbesi, subspecies of yellow-fronted parakeet

Cyanoramphus novaezelandiae, red-fronted parakeet

Pyrrhura cruentata, red-eared conure

Rhynchopsitta spp., thick-billed parrots (two races)

Strigops habroptilus, owl parrot or kakapo

Amazona arausiaca, red-necked Amazon

Amazona barabdensis, yellow-shouldered Amazon

Amazona brasiliensis, red-tailed Amazon

Amazona guildingii, St. Vincent Amazon

Amazona imperialis, imperial Amazon

Amazona leucocophala, Cuban Amazon

Amazona pretrei, red-spectacled Amazon

Amazon dufresniana rhodocorytha, red-crowned Amazon

Extinct Species

A number of parrots became extinct during the eighteenth and nineteenth centuries. The reasons are not known, but change in and destruction of the parrots' natural habitat have been blamed as well as shooting of the birds for food and catching them for the pet trade. The following list contains all the species that are known to have existed, and in parentheses the date when they presumably died out is given.

Nesto meridionalis productus, Norfolk Island kaka (1851)

Charmosyna diadema, New Caledonian lorikeet (ca. 1860)

Cyanoramphus zealandicus, black-footed parakeet (1844)

Cyanoramphus ulietanus, society parakeet (1773/4)

Cyanoramphus novaezelandiae subflavescens, subspecies of red-fronted parakeet (ca. 1870)

Cyanoramphus novaezelandiae erythrotis, subspecies of red-footed parakeet (1800-1820)

Mascarinus mascarinus, Mascarene parrot (1800-1820)

Psittacula eupatria wardi, Seychelles parakeet (ca. 1870)

Psittacula exsul, Newton's parakeet (ca. 1875)

Loriculus philippensis chrysonotus, subspecies of Philippine hanging parrot (after 1926)

Amazona vittata gracilipes, (subspecies of Puerto Rican Amazon (1899)

Aratinga chloroptera maugei, Mauge's conure (ca. 1860)

Conuropsis carolinensis carolinensis, Carolina parakeet (ca. 1900)

Conuropsis carolinensis ludovicianus, subspecies of the above (1914)

Ara tricolor, Cuban macaw (1885)

Useful Literature and Addresses

Books

Birmelin, I. and Wolter, A. (1985) *The New Parakeet Handbook,* Barron's Educational Series, Hauppauge, New York.

Cayley N.W., and Lendon, A. (1973). *Australian Parrots in Field and Aviary,* Angus & Robertson, Sydney, Australia.

Diemer, P. (1983). *Parrots,* Barron's Educational Series, Hauppauge, New York.

Eastman, W.R., and Hunt, A. C. (1966). *The Parrots of Australia,* Angus & Robertson, Sydney, Australia.

Forshaw, J.M. (1981). *Australian Parrots,* 2nd edition, Lansdowne Press, Melbourne, Australia.

(1978). *Parrots of the World,* 2nd edition, Lansdowne Press, Melbourne, Australia.

Harman, I. (1981). *Australian Parrots in Bush and Aviary,* Inkata Press, Melbourne and Sydney, Australia.

Lantermann, W. (1986), *The New Parrot Handbook,* Barron's Educational Series, Hauppauge, New York.

Low, R. (1989). *The Complete Book of Parrots,* Barron's Educational Series, Hauppauge, New York.

— (1984). *Endangered Parrots,* Blandford Press, Poole, Dorset, England.

— (1980). *Parrots, Their Care and Breeding,* Blandford Press, Poole, Dorset, England.

Moizer, S. and B. (1988). *The Complete Book of Budgerigars,* Barron's Educational Series, Hauppauge, New York.

Petrak, M.L. (1982). *Diseases of Cage and Aviary Birds,* 2nd edition, Lea & Febiger, Philadelphia.

Ruthers, A., and Norris, K.A. (1972). *Encyclopedia of Aviculture,* Vol. 2, Blandford Press, Poole, Dorset, England.

Vriends, M. M. (1986). *Lovebirds,* Barron's Educational Series, Hauppauge, New York.

—(1985). *The Macdonald Encyclopedia of Cage and Aviary Birds,* Macdonald & Co., Publishers, Ltd., London and Sydney, Australia.

—(1984). *Popular Parrots,* 2nd edition, Howell Book House, Inc., New York.

—(1986). *Simon and Schuster's Guide to Pet Birds,* Simon and Schuster, New York.

Wolter, A. *African Gray Parrots,* (1987), Barron's Educational Series, Hauppauge, New York.

Periodicals

American Cage Bird Magazine (Monthly; One Glamore Court, Smithtown, New York 11787)

Avicultural Bulletin (Monthly; Avicultural Society of America, Inc., P.O. Box 2796, Dept. CB, Redondo Beach, CA 90278)

Avicultural Magazine (Quarterly; The Avicultural Society, Windsor, Forest Stud, Mill Ride, Ascot, Berkshire, England)

Cage and Aviary Birds (Weekly; Prospect House, 9-15 Ewell Road, Cheam, Sutton, Surrey, SM3 8BZ, England); young birdkeepers under 16 may like to join the *Junior Bird League*; full details can be obtained from the J.B.L., *c/o Cage and Aviary Birds*

Magazine of the Parrot Society (Monthly; 19a De Parys Ave., Bedford, Bedfordshire, England)

Parrotworld (Monthly; National Parrot Association, 8 North Hoffman Lane, Hauppauge, New York 11788)

Watchbird (Bi-monthly; American Federation of Aviculture, P.O. Box 1568, Redondo Beach, CA 90278)

Useful Literature and Addresses

American Bird Clubs

Avicultural Society of America (see *Avicultural Bulletin*)

American Federation of Aviculture, Inc. (see *The A.F.A. Watchbird*)

National Parrot Association (see *Parrotworld*)

Australian Bird Clubs

Avicultural Society of Australia, c/o Mr. I.C.L. Jackson, Box 130, Broadford, Victoria 3658

Avicultural Society of Queensland, 19 Fahey's Road, Albany Creek, Queensland, 4035

Canadian Bird Clubs

Avicultural Advancement Council, P.O. Box 5126, Postal Station "B", Victoria, British Columbia, V8R 6N4

British Columbia Avicultural Society, c/o Mr. Paul Prior, 11784-90th Avenue, North Delta, British Columbia, V4C 3H6

Calgary and District Avicultural Society, c/o Mr. Richard Kary, 7728 Bowcliffe Cr., N.W. Calgary, Alberta, T3B 2S5

Canadian Parrot Association, Pine Oaks, R.R. Nr. 3, St. Catherines, Ontario, L2R 6P9

English Bird Clubs

The Avicultural Society (see *Avicultural Magazine*)

The Parrot Society (see *Magazine of the Parrot Society*)

New Zealand Bird Club

The Avicultural Society of New Zealand Inc., P.O. Box 21403, Henderson, Auckland 8

Veterinarian Association

Association of Avian Veterinarians, P.O. Box 299, East Northport, New York 11731

Index

Index

Index

Preening, 44
Psittacosis, 8, 33–34
Pumpkin seeds, 27

Quarantine period, 8, 56

Rearing, 40
Red-crowned Amazon, *10*, 53
Red-lored Amazon, *9*, 53–54
Regurgitated food, 40
Respiratory ailments, 32–33
Rice, 27
Room aviaries, 15
   placement of, 15

Salvin's Amazon, *19*
Scarlet Ara, *37*
Sex determination, 12
Sexual maturity, 6
Shelter, outdoor, 16–17
Shower bath, 23
Sick bird, 30
Single bird, 6, 22, 33

Smuggled birds, 13
Social preening, 44
Species preservation, 35
Spectacled Amazon parrot, 52
Speech training, 21–22
Sprouted feed, 27
Stones, for digestion, 14
Sunflower seeds, 27

Tapeworms, 32
Temperature, maintenance, 39
Thistle, 27
Threadworms, 32
Threatening behavior, 46
Threats, 13
Traveling cage, 18

U.S. Dept. of Agriculture, 55
U.S. Dept. of the Interior, 56
U.S. Public Health Service, 8

Vacation care, 7
Veterinarian, 31

Vinaceous Amazon, *47*
Vitamins, 28

Walnuts, 27
Washington Endangered Species
   Convention, 5, 12–13, 35
Wheat, 27
White-browed Amazon, 52
White-fronted Amazon, 12, 20,
   47, 52
White seed, 27
Wild plants, 28
Wings, 11

Yellow-cheeked Amazon, *19*, 47
Yellow-crowned Amazon, *19*,
   51–52
Yellow-headed Amazon, 47
Yellow-lored Amazon, 12
Yellow-naped Amazon, *37*
Yellow-necked Amazon, *38*
Young bird, 11

Perfect for Pet Owners!

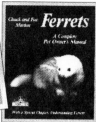

PET OWNER'S MANUALS

Over 50 illustrations per book (20 or more color photos), 72–80 pp., paperback.

ABYSSINIAN CATS
AFRICAN GRAY PARROTS
AMAZON PARROTS
BANTAMS
BEAGLES
BEEKEEPING
BOSTON TERRIERS
BOXERS
CANARIES
CATS
CHINCHILLAS
CHOW-CHOWS
CICHLIDS
COCKATIELS
COCKER SPANIELS
COCKATOOS
COLLIES
CONURES
DACHSHUNDS
DALMATIANS
DISCUS FISH
DOBERMAN PINSCHERS
DOGS
DOVES
DWARF RABBITS
ENGLISH SPRINGER SPANIELS
FEEDING AND SHELTERING BACKYARD
  BIRDS
FEEDING AND SHELTERING EUROPEAN
  BIRDS
FERRETS
GERBILS
GERMAN SHEPHERDS
GOLDEN RETRIEVERS
GOLDFISH
GOULDIAN FINCHES
GREAT DANES
GUINEA PIGS
GUPPIES, MOLLIES, AND PLATTIES
HAMSTERS
HEDGEHOGS
IRISH SETTERS
KEESHONDEN
KILLIFISH
LABRADOR RETRIEVERS
LHASA APSOS
LIZARDS IN THE TERRARIUM
LONGHAIRED CATS

LONG-TAILED PARAKEETS
LORIES AND LORIKEETS
LOVEBIRDS
MACAWS
MICE
MUTTS
MYNAHS
PARAKEETS
PARROTS
PERSIAN CATS
PIGEONS
POMERANIANS
PONIES
POODLES
POT BELLIES AND OTHER MINIATURE PIGS
PUGS
RABBITS
RATS
ROTTWEILERS
SCHNAUZERS
SCOTTISH FOLD CATS
SHAR-PEI
SHEEP
SHETLAND SHEEPDOGS
SHIH TZUS
SIAMESE CATS
SIBERIAN HUSKIES
SMALL DOGS
SNAKES
SPANIELS
TROPICAL FISH
TURTLES
WEST HIGHLAND WHITE TERRIERS
YORKSHIRE TERRIERS
ZEBRA FINCHES

NEW PET HANDBOOKS

Detailed, illustrated profiles (40–60 color photos), 144 pp., paperback.

NEW AQUARIUM FISH HANDBOOK
NEW AUSTRALIAN PARAKEET
  HANDBOOK
NEW BIRD HANDBOOK
NEW CANARY HANDBOOK
NEW CAT HANDBOOK
NEW COCKATIEL HANDBOOK
NEW DOG HANDBOOK
NEW DUCK HANDBOOK
NEW FINCH HANDBOOK

NEW GOAT HANDBOOK
NEW PARAKEET HANDBOOK
NEW PARROT HANDBOOK
NEW RABBIT HANDBOOK
NEW SALTWATER AQUARIUM
  HANDBOOK
NEW SOFTBILL HANDBOOK
NEW TERRIER HANDBOOK

REFERENCE BOOKS

Comprehensive, lavishly illustrated references (60–300 color photos), 136–176 pp., hardcover & paperback.

AQUARIUM FISH
AQUARIUM FISH BREEDING
AQUARIUM FISH SURVIVAL MANUAL
AQUARIUM PLANTS MANUAL
BEFORE YOU BUY THAT PUPPY
BEST PET NAME BOOK EVER, THE
CARING FOR YOUR SICK CAT
CAT CARE MANUAL
CIVILIZING YOUR PUPPY
COMMUNICATING WITH YOUR DOG
COMPLETE BOOK OF BUDGERIGARS
COMPLETE BOOK OF CAT CARE
COMPLETE BOOK OF DOG CARE
DOG CARE MANUAL
FEEDING YOUR PET BIRD
GOLDFISH AND ORNAMENTAL CARP
GUIDE TO A WELL-BEHAVED CAT
GUIDE TO HOME PET GROOMING
HEALTHY CAT, HAPPY CAT
HEALTHY DOG, HAPPY DOG
HOP TO IT: A Guide to Training Your Pet
  Rabbit
HORSE CARE MANUAL
HOW TO TALK TO YOUR CAT
HOW TO TEACH YOUR OLD DOG
  NEW TRICKS
LABYRINTH FISH
NONVENOMOUS SNAKES
TROPICAL MARINE FISH
  SURVIVAL MANUAL

Barron's Educational Series, Inc. • 250 Wireless Blvd., Hauppauge, NY 11788
Call toll-free: 1-800-645-3476 • In Canada: Georgetown Book Warehouse
34 Armstrong Ave., Georgetown, Ont. L7G 4R9 • Call toll-free: 1-800-247-7160
Order from your favorite book or pet store.

(#62) R 2/97